ATE DUE

WITHDRAWN

SAMUEL COLERIDGE-TAYLOR

Anglo-Black Composer, 1875-1912

by

William Tortolano

The Scarecrow Press, Inc.
Metuchen, N.J.   1977

Portions of Chapter One are adapted by permission
from the author's article, "Samuel Coleridge-Taylor
1875-1912," Music / The AGO and RCCO Magazine,
August 1975, pp25-27.

The poems, "Compensation," "A Love Song," and "A
Negro Love Song," are from The Complete Poems
of Paul Laurence Dunbar, copyright 1913 by Dodd,
Mead & Co., and are reprinted by permission.

A review by Richard Aldrich, in his Concert Life
in New York, 1902-1923 (New York: G. P. Putnam's Sons, copyright © 1941 by Richard Aldrich),
pp155-156, is reprinted in Chapter Five by permission of the publisher.

A portion of an article, "Some Notes on Samuel
Coleridge-Taylor," by Herbert Antcliffe, which appeared in The Musical Quarterly, 1922, pp184-
185, is reprinted in Chapter Five by permission
of the publisher.

An article by Coleridge-Taylor, "Is Technique
Strangling Beauty?" is reprinted in Chapter Seven
by permission, from the Etude Music Magazine,
January 1911, copyright © 1911 by the Theodore
Presser Company.

Library of Congress Cataloging in Publication Data

Tortolano, William.
      Samuel Coleridge-Taylor : Anglo-Black composer,
   1875-1912.

780.92
C693t   "Catalog of music by Coleridge-Taylor": p.
           Discography: p.
           Bibliography: p.
1977   Includes index.
           1. Coleridge-Taylor, Samuel, 1875-1912.
      2. Composers--England--Biography.
      ML410.C74T7   780'.92'4 [B]   76-57172
      ISBN 0-8108-1010-7

Dedicated to my good friend
Dr. Richard Marlow
of Trinity College, Cambridge

TABLE OF CONTENTS

ACKNOWLEDGMENTS

Dr. Richard Marlow, Trinity College, Cambridge, England, kindly read the text in its early stages. Dr. Marlow not only gave encouragement but made arrangements for the author to spend the Easter term, 1974, as a member of the High Table at Trinity. Dr. Peter LeHuray also very kindly invited the author to spend the Easter term, 1974, as a member of the High Table at St. Catharine's College, Cambridge. This term was devoted to research on Coleridge-Taylor and the kindness of these two scholars is greatly appreciated.

Avril Coleridge-Taylor, daughter of the great composer, was pleased with the author's article on her father in Music / The AGO-RCCO Magazine. Needless to say, her knowledge of the composer is personal and her observations were of help.

Dr. Mildred Ellis of Washington, D. C. , not only kept up an encouraging correspondence but patiently made up lists of Coleridge-Taylor music held by the Library of Congress and by Howard University for the author.

John D. Donoghue, Joseph Sullivan and Dr. Edward Murphy very kindly read the text and offered valuable suggestions regarding style. Members of the library staff at the Royal College of Music, London, also were very helpful.

INTRODUCTION

There are several composers and musical personalities of distinction and individuality that have somehow escaped the attention of historians. Samuel Coleridge-Taylor was a very popular and important composer during his short lifetime. Although performances of his music continued for some time after his death, they gradually lost momentum. Today he is rarely performed, seldom referred to in history books and little known. What happened and why?

Coleridge-Taylor had a great talent, a unique personal style, fine craftsmanship in his harmony and orchestral color, eminently singable melodies and rhythmic strength. The same attributes can be applied to other composers. But much of his music is related to his Negro background. An Anglo-Black composer is in itself a rarity, but when a composer of his talent arrives at a particularly opportune moment of history, a cultural renaissance is a potential. This potential was realized through his imaginative and distinctive use of Negro melody and rhythm from Africa and in particular from the United States. Coleridge-Taylor was so inspired by American Negro music and poetry that he in turn through musical compositions became a leader and shining light to an American Negro cultural renaissance. There is no other historical incident of this type.

It worked both ways. The 1890's and the period prior to World War I saw the emergence of many Negro leaders, artists, musicians and educators. Some social theories advocated a return of the Black man from the United States to Africa. Others saw recognition and fulfillment in the expression of inherent and indigenous arts. Some of the outstanding personalities of this epoch were W. E. B. DuBois, the great social reformer; Booker T. Washington, educator and practical man; the Fisk Jubilee Singers and Harry T. Burleigh, advocates of the Negro spiritual; and Paul Laurence Dunbar, poet of both conventional language and Negro dialect. There were other names, of course. But these stand out as luminaries. All of them were inspired by the example of Samuel Coleridge-Taylor, for here was a man who achieved international artistic fame and who used his own ethnic heritage in musical composition. He was both a model and an inspiration.

Coleridge-Taylor had to overcome many social prejudices. Born of a white mother and a black father, he was indeed part of a small minority, often despised and misunderstood. Later in life, he married a white woman and this was also to present him with manifestations of prejudice. But somehow he was able to overcome all this. He had talent. It was a beautiful talent that often expressed rich melodies from the Negro heritage. Coleridge-Taylor spoke through his music. We find very few examples of writings, letters to editors, or articles that are ethnically protective or provocative. The composer wanted to do for Negro folk music what his contemporaries Grieg, Brahms and Dvořák had done for Norwegian, Hungarian and Bohemian folk music. Although Coleridge-Taylor was a black nationalist in the sense that he employed ethnic material, he was also very British. He was educated and spent his life in England.

It all seems so long ago, yet it is not. There are

still a few people alive who remember Coleridge-Taylor, including his son and daughter. The son, Hiawatha, was almost 12 when his father died, and the daughter, Avril (Gwendolyn) was 9.

The availability of the music is problematic and frus-
trating. It is important of course to study each and every
composition. The music has been over the years increasing-
ly difficult to come by, yet it was popular and widely available a generation or two ago, when Coleridge-Taylor was
fashionable. For most he is now out of vogue and there is
also the current popularity of Scott Joplin's (and others')
rags, which, musically, took an approach opposite to that of
Coleridge-Taylor. (They were contemporaries and although
there is no evidence that they knew one another, we do know
that Coleridge-Taylor knew the rag music of the time. He,
as well as DuBois and Burleigh, had contempt for this type
of musical expression, for they felt that the spiritual was the
true manifestation of the American Negro.) One can find
some of Coleridge-Taylor's music on occasion in antiquarian music shops. But it is quite difficult to purchase the
man's entire musical literature.

The music is available for study at the British Museum.
There is also an extensive amount at the University Library
at Cambridge and good-sized holdings at the Library of Congress, the Boston Public Library and the New York Public
Library. Most of these are the original editions. Original
manuscripts, letters and other personal memorabilia are dis-
persed. But probably the latest assembled and largest collection of manuscripts can be found at the Royal College of
Music, London. Many are recent acquisitions from the
daughter.

The frustrations and problems of writing a book on

the life and music of Samuel Coleridge-Taylor are many.
The music is hard to find. First-hand personal mementoes
and recollections are equally difficult to find. The two children are both living in England. Although the author had
several gracious letters from the daughter, when he went on
a research visit to England for the express purpose of writing about the composer, she was too busy to see him. The
son, after some correspondence, seemed to lose interest in
a television production in the United States projected for 1975,
the centenary of the composer's birth. The author is appre-
ciative to the daughter, Avril Coleridge-Taylor, for her words
of encouragement in his research. Her observations, based
on personal knowledge, were helpful, even though most of
her information about her father was guarded from outsider's
use.

The approach in this book is first to try to make
Coleridge-Taylor known as a significant composer so he can
be given his rightful place in history. The composer's im-
pact upon the Negro community in the United States continued
for years after his death in 1912. The writings of Negro
leaders of this time should be read again and their accom-
plishments evaluated for their role in the life and music of
Coleridge-Taylor. It is also hoped that many of his musical
compositions will again find their proper places in concert
literature or at least that they will be recognized as works
of historical and musicological importance. The choral music
includes not only the ever-fresh and imaginative Song of Hiawatha, but other fine works such as Meg Blane, Five Choral
Ballads (Longfellow), and A Tale of Old Japan. The ethnic
orchestral music includes The African Suite, The Bamboula,
Toussaint L'Ouverture, Ethiopia Saluting the Colours and Symphonic Variations on an African Air. He also composed ex-

cellent chamber music, anthems, songs, operas, incidental music to plays, and solo pieces. A catalogue of Coleridge-Taylor's music, together with cross references, is also part of this book.

Although Samuel Coleridge-Taylor was a minor composer, he was a major figure within that class of highly gifted and talented composers who leave an important imprint upon their fellow artists, an ethnic heritage and a musical style. Much of that music deserves to be heard again. Perhaps Coleridge-Taylor will not escape history.

Chapter One

SCHOOLING AND EARLY CAREER

Samuel Coleridge-Taylor was an unusual and gifted composer and an important figure during his lifetime. Indeed, his choral trilogy, Scenes from the Song of Hiawatha, rivaled that of his admired contemporary, Sir Edward Elgar, composer of The Dream of Gerontius. Coleridge-Taylor's position in Victorian England was distinctive, perhaps unique. It is not possible to separate the man's background from the music he composed or to ignore the very unusual situation of an Anglo-Negro in the mainstream of British musical life exerting an unmistakable influence upon his Negro brethren in the United States.

No English Negro ever played such an important role in the musical life of his country as did Samuel Coleridge-Taylor. It is in fact difficult to find any composer of this particular background in English music. A minor exception might be Fela Sowande, 1905-1973, who was born in Nigeria, but lived in England. Although Sowande can claim British citizenship, he did not have the influence that Coleridge-Taylor had upon musical life in England.

Samuel Coleridge-Taylor was born in Holborn, London, on August 15, 1875. His father was Dr. Daniel Hughes Taylor, a West African Negro from Sierra Leone who came to England to continue his schooling at Taunton College, Somerset, and later at King's University College in London as a

medical student. He is described as being short, neat and
fastidious in his taste and appearance; charming and intelli-
gent. Eventually he became a member of the Royal College
of Surgeons and a licentiate of the Royal College of Physicians.

Little is known about his life and work. The young
doctor became an assistant to a Croydon medical doctor and
evidently enjoyed success. The white patients seemed to like
the young assistant with such gracious manners and happy
demeanor. Eventually he sought a practice of his own but
this became disastrous because of resentment of his color.
As an assistant he was received with little reservation, but
as an independent doctor he was mistrusted. Dr. Taylor returned to Africa around 1876. It is known that he held several appointments in West Africa including that of acting
assistant colonial surgeon and acting civil commandant of
British Sherbro. Later he set up private practice in Sierra
Leone, but met with financial disappointment. His name appeared in the Foreign List of the Medical Directory from
1877 to 1882.

The young Samuel was encouraged to write to his father. But evidently the elder never answered. He contributed
little if anything to his wife's and son's support. According
to W. C. Berwick Sayers, the first biographer of the composer (Samuel Coleridge-Taylor, Musician; His Life and Letters, London: Cassell, 1915), Dr. Taylor's death was re-
ported in West African papers as having taken place in Bath-
urst, the Gambia.

The matter of the mother of Samuel Coleridge-Taylor
is enigmatic. Sayers relates in his biography that the young
doctor visited a home in which a young woman, Alice Howe,
lived as a lady's companion and friend. She was about 17
years old. They were attracted to one another and a secret

marriage was planned. Alice evidently had no reservations about their differences in skin color.

Since the young student had little money, they settled with a working family by the name of Holman at 15 Theobald's Square, Red Lion Square, Holborn (London). On August 15, 1875, a son was born. He was named after the great English poet.

There appears to be a certain mystery as to who was actually his mother. Percy Young ("Samuel Coleridge-Taylor, 1875-1912," Musical Times (London), Aug. 1975, p703) raises this question. The birth certificate issued on September 27, 1875, listed the mother as Alice Holmans. An obituary notice for Coleridge-Taylor himself in the Neue Musik-Zeitung (1912) stated the mother's name as Josten. A personal letter from the daughter of the composer to the author also has reservations. A recent article (William Tortolano, "Samuel Coleridge-Taylor," Music / The AGO and RCCO Magazine, Aug. 1975, p25) had stated that the young doctor "married a handsome English woman." Miss Coleridge-Taylor, the daughter, wrote, "But we don't know this. For the real mother of Coleridge-Taylor is not known." Jessie F. Coleridge-Taylor, wife of the composer, makes no such enigmatic remarks in her book (Genius and Musician, London: privately printed, 1943). Her only remark is, "Many people will doubtless recall Coleridge-Taylor's deep love for his mother which was indeed a wonderful example of devotion. She married an Englishman after Dr. Taylor's death, but her son continued to help her up to the time of his death."

Coleridge-Taylor's mother's photograph is in the Sayers book. She is indeed handsome. The composer always spoke fondly of her. The mother lived with the Holman family until Samuel was about five years old in what

were probably very humble circumstances. She undertook a
second marriage to a Mr. Evans. Although their circumstances were limited, the marriage offered a new home for
mother and son at Wodden New Road, where the young man
lived until 1894.

Young Coleridge-Taylor's religious convictions were
strong. As a youngster, he was a chorister in Presbyterian
and Anglican Churches, often appearing as a soprano soloist.
His biographer and lifelong friend, W. C. Berwick Sayers,
mentions that Taylor "rarely discussed his beliefs, but he
had a sure instinct for the Hereafter, and his life was essentially a religious one. I do not know what his creed was,
but at the back of everything he did--even his minor works
--lay a strong religious feeling" (Samuel Coleridge-Taylor,
1915, p97).

Coleridge-Taylor was very proud of his color. It
was common practice in England at the time, and still ap-
propriate, to refer to blacks as "coloured"; "Negro" was also used quite often. "Black" was seldom used. Nevertheless, the book, The Souls of Black Folk (1904) by W. E. B.
DuBois, profoundly influenced the young composer and
"black" became a relevant word for him. The composer's
daughter, who is British, raises the question of the use of
"coloured" and "Black" in a letter to the author: "I notice
you use the word Black ... instead of 'coloured' as my
father always referred to himself and his coloured friends."

Coleridge-Taylor hated the early criticisms which
dealt with his skin and his music. At first he saw little
difference. He felt he was a British musician with an English education. But his skin color soon became intensely
meaningful to him as an expression of his deep love and
commitment to his brethren. This was manifested in many

compositions that utilize ethnic poetry about Negroes, such as Henry Wadsworth Longfellow's Poems of Slavery. It is illustrated also in musical works that use African melodies and rhythms. But it is outstanding when he assimilates American Negro melodies into his music.

On his death bed, Coleridge-Taylor expressed a fear to his wife, "When I die, the critics will call me a Creole." He wanted to be a Negro musician.

The composer wanted to serve Negro folk music. He has often been criticized for his lack of classical forms, such as the sonata and the symphonic, and his lack of contrapuntal techniques. But these forms would be largely artificial and difficult to impose upon his melodic and harmonic ideas. For this reason, he turned to folk music and its metamorphoses. The young composer first heard American Negro spirituals sung by a Negro choir in the late nineties. The famous Fisk Jubilee Singers visited England with their manager, Frederick J. Loudin. Coleridge-Taylor attended some of the concerts and was deeply affected by not only the authenticity of the musical material but the distinctive vocal timbre. From this point on Negro melodies recur frequently in his work.

He composed a provocative ethnic repertoire which includes a set of songs, African Romances; Ethiopia Saluting the Colours, op. 51, a concert march for full orchestra; Four African Dances, op. 58, for violin and piano; and Symphonic Variations on an African Air, op. 63, for orchestra. Of particular success and beauty is his Twenty-Four Negro Melodies, op. 59, no. 1, for piano, which are mainly sacred folk songs and spirituals from the United States and Africa.

Coleridge-Taylor gained valuable initial material not only from the Fisk Jubilee Singers but from a fortunate early friendship with Paul Laurence Dunbar (1872-1906), the poet and first Negro to gain a national reputation in the United States. He was also the first to use Negro dialect in his poetry. A man of strength and complete dedication to his race, he had a great influence in shaping the destiny of the composer.

In 1896, Dunbar completed Lyrics of Lowly Life, which brought him his fame and established his reputation. His later works included Lyrics of Love and Laughter (1903), Lyrics of Sunshine and Shadow (1905), and Complete Poems, published posthumously in 1913. His short, tragic life and bitter destiny is effectively summed up in his poem "Compensation" from Lyrics of Sunshine and Shadow (New York: Dodd, Mead, 1905):

> Because I had loved so deeply,
> Because I had loved so long,
> God in His great compassion,
> Gave me the gift of song.
> Because I have loved so vainly,
> And sung with such faltering breath,
> The Master in infinite mercy
> Offers the boon of Death.

Coleridge-Taylor's fame was already established in America in 1896. Many Negroes looked to him with anticipation and expectation for the future. In that year, Dunbar visited England in order to give public readings of his poetry and eagerly sought out Coleridge-Taylor. The result was several outstanding joint recitals, the composer playing several of his compositions and Dunbar reading his poetry. Several of Dunbar's lyrics were set to music by Coleridge-Taylor and Hiawathan Sketches for violin and piano were

also given--evidence of an early infatuation with the Longfellow poem. Coleridge-Taylor was a very fine violinist, thanks
to the solid training in technique given him as a boy by Joseph Beckwith.

Coleridge-Taylor used poetry by Dunbar in composing
his African Romances, op. 17. Together with two short
poems by Dunbar, "Candle Lightin' Time" and "A Corn
Song," these were his first compositions to use inspiration
from his own race. None of the poems in African Romances
specifically refers to Africa, but the young composer saw in
them romance and ethnic identity.

Dunbar also collaborated with the composer on another
early opus (25), Dream Lovers, an operatic romance for two
male and two female characters, chorus and orchestra. Although his African Suite, op. 35, was originally for pianoforte solo, it was also inspired by the poet. The second of
the four movements is called "A Negro Love Song," the
first poem in dialect to be used by Coleridge-Taylor. The
suite also contains the energetic "Danse Nègre" which is
equally effective as an orchestral work in the composer's
own arrangement.

The title for "A Love Song" was changed in the musical version to "An African Love Song" and became the
first of seven Dunbar poems used by Coleridge-Taylor in
African Romances, op. 17. It was originally published in
Lyrics of Love and Laughter (New York: Dodd, Mead, 1903).

"A Love Song"

Ah, love, my love is like a cry in the night,
A long, loud cry to the empty sky,
The cry of a man alone in the desert,
With hands uplifted, with parching lips,

Oh, rescue me, rescue me,
Thy form to mine arms,
The dew of thy lips to my mouth,
Dost thou hear me?-my call thro' the night?

Darling, I hear thee and answer,
Thy fountain am I,
All of the love of my soul will I bring to thee
All of the pains of my being shall wring to thee,
Deep and forever the song of my loving shall sing to thee,
Ever and ever thro' day and thro' night shall I cling to thee.
Hearest thou the answer?
Darling, I come, I come.

A Negro Love Song, in dialect, was the inspiration
for African Suite, op. 35, and comes from Lyrics of Lowly
Life (New York: Dodd, Mead, 1896).

"A Negro Love Song"

Seen my lady home las' night,
    Jump back, honey, jump back.
Hel' hun han' an' sque'z it tight,
    Jump back, honey, jump back.
Hyeahd huh sigh a little sigh,
Seen a light gleam f'om huh eye,
An' a smile go flittin' by--
    Jump back, honey, jump back.

Hyeahd de win' blow thoo de pine,
    Jump back, honey, jump back.
Mockin'-bird was singin' fine,
    Jump back, honey, jump back.
An' my hea't was beatin' so,
When I reached my lady's do',
Dat I couldn't ba' to go--
    Jump back, honey, jump back.

Put my ahm aroun' huh wais',
    Jump back, honey, jump back.
Raised huh lips an' took a tase,
    Jump back, honey, jump back.
Love me, honey, love me true?
Love me well ez I love You?
An' she answe'd, "'Cose I do"--
    Jump back, honey, jump back.

Coleridge-Taylor shortly before his marriage.

Marriage

Jessie S. Fleetwood Walmisley and Samuel Coleridge-Taylor fell in love as students at the Royal College of Music. The pangs of frustration at the bitter prejudice surrounding the composer deeply affected her. She loved him and his Negro background had absolutely no bearing. But her family and many friends could not understand the love between a white woman and a black man.

The youth followed the honorable old course of calling on her family to ask their consent to the engagement. He was rejected by the family. "You will now have to act without your family," he told Jessie.

The morning before the marriage, Jessie's mother said, "Your father and I would like to shake hands with Coleridge-Taylor before you are married." The composer was generous and forgiving. There was a happy relationship from that time on.

Samuel and Jessie were married, quietly, on December 30, 1899, at Holy Trinity Church, South Norwood. On the wedding day the bride received a telegram from her groom:

> You shall enter in my wigwam for the
> heart's right hand I gave you.
>
> Hiawatha.

And they never did leave one another. Coleridge-Taylor told a dear friend,

> I have been very happy in my surroundings all my life, first in my mother and then in my marriage. Even without any moderate success I think I should have been one of those rare beings--a happy man. Unlike a great many painters, and barristers who want to be journalists, I want to be nothing in the world except what I am--a musician.

When the composer died his widow buried all their personal letters and evidently had never discussed them with anyone.

His Children

Hiawatha Coleridge-Taylor was born in London, October 3, 1900, and became a conductor, active in the performance of his father's music. It was very popular in the 1920's and 1930's to stage large-scale musical productions of various Coleridge-Taylor works, particularly Hiawatha. The son's most conspicuous appearances were as the conductor of these scenic productions, often at the Royal Albert Hall. The first took place on May 19, 1924; young Coleridge-Taylor conducted the pageant-opera production of Hiawatha.

Avril Coleridge-Taylor (born Gwendolyn) is well known in her own right as a composer and conductor. She was born in London on March 8, 1903. Her studies included violin with Joseph Ivimey, orchestration with Gordon Jacob, composition with Alec Rowley, and conducting with Ernest Read and Albert Coates. A distinguished conductor, Miss Coleridge-Taylor has appeared as the guest head of the Band of H. M. Royal Marines; the BBC Symphony, Concert and Theatre Orchestras; the South African Broadcasting Co. 's Orchestra; and the London Symphony.

In addition to many arrangements of her father's music, Miss Coleridge-Taylor has herself been a prolific composer. In 1957 she wrote the Ceremonial March to mark Ghana's Independence. This composition was broadcast by the BBC Scottish Orchestra and the Ghana Broadcasting Service during Harold Macmillan's visit to Ghana.

Coleridge-Taylor's wife in her book (Genius and Musician, 1943) relates that she was tormented about the results of mixed marriages, particularly before the birth of the first child. Her first question to the doctor the day Hiawatha was born was "is he black, white, red or yellow?" The doctor was quite taken but replied, "Good gracious, he's none of these--a beautiful boy."

The parents had originally hoped for a girl and had selected Barbara as a name. But Hiawatha seemed like the inevitable choice. The girl who came three years later was named Gwendolyn. The Coleridge-Taylors were in South Wales, where he was adjudicating a choral competition some months before the birth of the girl. The Welsh name was suggested by Lady William, the wife of Queen Victoria's physician and a friend of the new parents.

Musical Influences

In addition to the strong influence of Negro music from both Africa and the United States, Samuel Coleridge-Taylor found inspiration in several nationalistic composers with whom he seemed to identify. At first they seem like odd choices: Grieg, and particularly Dvořák. He seemed to dislike Moussorgsky and the Russian Nationalists. One might ask why didn't he select Bach, Mozart or Beethoven and other classical masters. It was, of course, the ethnic spirit and use of folk melody that dominated his thinking. Dvořák in particular seemed to have the empathy he needed. He was about 17 when he became possessed of complete devotion to Dvořák, which if anything, only increased with the years. Coleridge-Taylor showed an unabashed love of pure melody, its metamorphosis, and harmonic and orchestral color.

Brahms was also an important model to him.   All
music students are familiar with the intense feelings of musicians during this era regarding the rivalry between admir-
ers of Wagner and Brahms.   In England similar feelings
were also engendered over the rival influences of Sir Charles
Villiers Stanford and Sir Edward Elgar (and also Cambridge
and Oxford universities).   Brahms was an idol and model
for Stanford pupils and Coleridge-Taylor naturally fell under
Brahms' influence too.   There is an interesting story that
Stanford asked his composition class to compose a clarinet
quintet, such as Brahms had done--but "to keep it clear of
Brahms."   Coleridge-Taylor's quintet enjoyed critical ac-
claim, even though some writers found the influence of
Brahms very evident in the style.

Although Elgar was not an obvious model for Coleridge-
Taylor, both composed in the oratorio genre popular in England at the time.   Sir Edward was a good friend of the younger man and greatly admired his talent.

The 15-year-old musician began his studies at the
Royal College of Music with the Christmas term of 1890.
He was shy almost to the point of personal terror.   He
made a few lifelong friends at the College, but on the whole
he was self-conscious and timid.   His principal teachers
were Dr. Charles Wood in harmony and Sir Walter Parratt.
Although he enrolled in violin and made excellent progress,
his interest developed in composition, as evidenced through
an excellent anthem, "In Thee O Lord," written in 1891 and
published by Novello (who also brought out most of his other
sacred music) when he was but 16.   The six-page anthem
was dedicated to Col. Herbert A. Walters, who early cham-
pioned the young composer and financed his formal musical
education.   It is a well-constructed work, showing potential

for the future. Walters later remarked of it,

> It is a careful setting of the words, with broad suave
> passages, a promising appreciation of voice values,
> and a certain amount of colours. It is characteristic
> that this little work already shows what was conspicu-
> ous in all Coleridge-Taylor's subsequent writing, that
> he gave considerable attention to the right accentua-
> tion of the words, and would sacrifice his melody to
> correct interpretation rather than torture the words to
> fit a preconceived melody.

In the same year, in 1891, Walters wrote to Sir
George Grove, principal of the Royal College of Music, sug-
gesting that Coleridge-Taylor might be a worthy pupil of
Sir Charles Stanford. Grove concurred and immediately
made the necessary arrangements.

In 1892 four more of the young composer's anthems
were published by Novello. These showed bold harmonies
and fine phrasing. Two of them, "Break Forth into Joy,"
a Christmas anthem, and "The Lord Is My Strength," a
short anthem for Easter, were both based on chorales from
Hymns Ancient and Modern (ed. D. W. H. Monk, 1861,
rev. ed. 1875). The other two, "Lift Up Your Heads," a
short festival anthem, and "O Ye That Love the Lord,"
completed the set. They are still available. These are
audacious works, but well-suited for the voice, and show a
sensitive feeling for the words.

Coleridge-Taylor soon idolized his famous teacher.
Stanford possessed fine musicianship and a large fund of
general knowledge. In addition to his important teaching
duties at the Royal College, he enjoyed the intellectual atmosphere as organist and professor at Trinity College,
Cambridge. Stanford was evidently a methodical and thorough teacher who drilled his pupils in the logical order of
musical craftsmanship. Young Coleridge-Taylor's progress

was such that in March, 1893, he applied for one of the nine open scholarships at the college and was successful, thereby becoming a Scholar.

The period during which the composer studied at the Royal College was one of great brilliance there. In addition to the principalship of Sir George Grove (editor of Grove's Dictionary of Music), and teachers like Wood, Parratt, and Stanford, its students included many excellent future artists and composers. Ralph Vaughan Williams was one of these. Coleridge-Taylor's temperament was such, however, that he came into intimate contact with very few students (although one was Vaughan Williams).

The training was conservative, but solid. Coleridge-Taylor was to remain conservative in his musical thinking. One sees no influence upon him whatsoever of Stravinsky, Schönberg, or even Debussy, Ravel or Mahler. He did admire Puccini's sense of color. But modernists for him were to be Grieg, Dvořák and Brahms.

Sayers reports in his biography that Stanford indicated to him some remembrances of the young student during this period. Coleridge-Taylor was exemplary in his industry, was cheerful and showed unaffected gratitude. The student had many brilliant ideas but seemed to lack the power of sustaining them. Often his musical thoughts were repetitious, but nevertheless dramatically conceived. Stanford equated the sense of the dramatic with his Negro background. Sir Charles was himself a significant composer of sacred music and undoubtedly demanded of his pupils compositions of a sacred nature. (He certainly insisted on a solid background in harmony, counterpoint and logical compositional order from them.) In all, Coleridge-Taylor composed several pieces of sacred choral music--eight short

anthems, two service settings, a cantata (The Atonement),
and several short organ works. Five of the anthems are
mentioned above. A sixth, "By the Waters of Babylon" (published by Novello in 1899), is highly reminiscent of Dvořák's
same title in his Biblical Songs. They both feature a judi-
cious use of grace notes. In 1900 Coleridge-Taylor wrote
to his boyhood friend, W. Y. Hurlstone,

> I have been influenced by Dvořák--a bad choice you
> will probably say--for Dvořák's influence on the Eng-
> lish music generally has not been great.... Please
> remember that I do not advance this view as criti-
> cism. It is simply my personal predilection, and is
> possibly largely temperamental [Sayers, p98].

The remaining two anthems, "When Thou Has Given
Me" and "Now Late on the Sabbath Day," an Eastertide anthem, were both composed in 1901.

In addition to the anthems, Coleridge-Taylor also
composed two settings of church services before 1900. The
first, "Te Deum," was written possibly in 1890 when he was
15. Not published until 1921, it bears the sub-title, "a
simple setting for parish choirs." The second is a more
ambitious setting: the "Morning and Evening Service" in F,
op. 18, for mixed voices and organ, composed in 1899 and
contained in Novello's Parish Choir Book. The sections are
Te Deum laudamus, Benedictus, Jubilate Deo, Magnificat
and Nunc dimittis.

Coleridge-Taylor composed only three short compositions for the organ. All were written in 1908 for a Novello publication called The Village Organist. The titles are
indicative of the period: "Arietta in F," "Elegy in G Minor,"
"Melody in D." Much more fascinating are the enormous
number of "arrangements" for organ, many of which the
composer personally approved. Again, these reflect a

period when organists would play compositions that were originally written for another medium. These help provide provocative insights into the organ performance literature of the
day, and into social conventions as well. A recent example
of this practice by Coleridge-Taylor can be seen in his arrangement of "The Willow Song" from Shakespeare's Othello,
not published until 1970 by J. B. Cramer, Ltd., London, as
part of a collection entitled Cramer's Library of Organ Music by British Composers. This is an arrangement for the
organ of the original orchestral music by Coleridge-Taylor
for a 1910 production of Othello.

His Career

    Financial problems were always prevalent in the
Coleridge-Taylor household. He enjoyed great popularity as
a composer and was given several important commissions,
but he could never make enough money from royalties to live
on this alone. This is not unusual of course. But when we
think of the enormous popularity of Hiawatha and the tremendous profit it brought to its publishers, it is indeed quite
sad to learn that the composer received very little money
from it. It was the most popular English oratorio from 1898
to 1912. After one production of this rapidly famous work,
the following article was published in The Musical Times
(London), September 1, 1903, p591.

THE POSSIBILITIES OF MUSICAL DEVELOPMENT
AMONG COLOURED PEOPLE

    "The latent possibilities of musical development
among coloured people have long been discussed in
America, but public performances have generally been

limited to plantation melodies and coon songs. Some earnest-minded coloured people in Washington thought the time had arrived when the musical ability of their race should be put to the test. Accordingly in 1901 an organization was formed in the American capital for the production of a composition by a coloured composer, the famous 'Hiawatha' by Mr. S. Coleridge-Taylor. After nearly a year's steady rehearsal the Coleridge-Taylor Choral Society--that being the name of the organization above referred to--performed the 'Hiawatha' music on April 23 last in the Metropolitan Methodist Episcopal Church, Washington, with extraordinary success. The audience numbered 1,500 people, mostly coloured folk, though there was a good sprinkling of white listeners, and at the public rehearsal (for admission to which a reduced charge was made) nearly 3,000 people were turned away.

'None but coloured people took part in the performance--the faces of the soloists, chorus (numbering 175 singers in evening dress) and accompanists being of a dusky hue, while the able conductor, Mr. John T. Layton (well known as the efficient choir director of the church where the concert took place), is a coal-black, burly negro of the pure African type. As no qualified coloured orchestra players could be found it had originally been planned to secure the services of white performers, but the demands of 'Hiawatha' orchestration proved to be too much for those accustomed to play at dances and hotels; the accompaniments were therefore played on two pianofortes, at which Mrs. L. Europe and Mrs. Robert Pelham efficiently presided. The soloists were Mrs. Skeene-Mitchell, of Cleveland;

Mr. Sidney Woodward, of Florida; and Mr. Harry Burleigh, of New York.

"The chorus-singing was really excellent and deserving of all praise. Even several eminent white musicians have borne testimony to its high achievement, and even the white press acknowledge that the performance was a splendid success. Considering the deep-rooted racial feeling among the white and coloured people this is all the more gratifying and encouraging. Moreover we understand that it is the first time that white singers have applied in hundreds for admission to an entirely coloured Society (in U. S. A.) and have been refused admission because there was not room for them! The greatest credit is due first to Mr. Andrew W. Hilyer, who conceived the idea of the Society, and then to the conductor, Mr. John T. Layton, director of music in the coloured public schools of Washington, and to his enthusiastic singers. The concert opens up a field of interesting speculation as to the possibilities of coloured people in their interpretation of good music, and fully justifies the decision of the Society to continue their work as a permanent organization. We wish them every success in their artistic endeavours."

Despite favorable notices such as this, building up his artistic success, Coleridge-Taylor received only £15. 15s total as a financial reward. Consequently, the composer was forced to teach endless hours, adjudicate musical competitions for small fees in many parts of England and Wales and conduct not only his own compositions as guest conductor, but the standard repertoire with various amateur and semi-professional community orchestras. He did enjoy doing

all this to some extent, but these duties unquestionably dis-
tracted from the time necessary for composition and drew
heavily upon his energies.

His longest teaching position was at the Croydon Conservatoire of Music, which he joined in 1895. It presented
problems to him at first for he was still a student and the
local citizenry remembered him as a small coloured boy of
''negligible social antecedents in which Col. Walters had
taken an interest.'' He not only met these prejudices head
on but triumphed over them. Most of all, the Conservatoire
offered him the opportunity to conduct its orchestral ensemble,
thereby providing an excellent chance for the young conductor
to develop.

Among his teaching positions was a professorship in
composition at Trinity College of Music, London, which he
accepted in 1903 and held until his death. He sought to encourage individuality in the pupil, often restricting his criticisms to a student's overall effect.

In 1905 he accepted a further teaching position as professor of theory and harmony at the Crystal Palace School of
Art and Music in South London. His students were in general young ladies whom he would teach on Saturday mornings.
He was admired for his gentle attitude and generosity. In
addition, he taught at the Guildhall School from 1910 to 1912,
and, at various times, private pupils as well. He distributed
prizes to the students at the Streatham School of Music in
November, 1905. His talk (reprinted beginning on page 148)
is a clear exhortation for the well-rounded, complete musician.

Many contemporary accounts tell that although Coleridge-Taylor was not a great conductor, he was highly compe-
tent. He was often asked to conduct his own compositions,

particularly for the various choral festivals so popular in Great Britain.

The composer derived a great deal of satisfaction as director, beginning in 1898, of the Croydon Orchestral Society. The position was, of course, full of the problems inherent in the direction of any amateur group. The disadvantages grew heavy and ultimately he resigned the position in 1906; but before doing so he created a new ensemble, the Coleridge-Taylor Symphony Concerts. It consisted of his better string players and some imported players from London, and gave performances in the years 1902-1905. Financial obstacles soon were insurmountable, however, the result being a further dissolution and the creation of the String Players Club in 1906.

In addition to his Croydon conducting duties, Taylor held various other conducting positions, including the Rochester Choral Society (1902-07) and the Handel Society (1904-12), concurrently for several years. The Handel Society membership was made up from fashionable West London music lovers. It existed primarily to perpetuate its namesake, but Taylor gave his energies to modern music. He regarded the 17th-century composer as crude and bare and was irritated by what he felt was plagiarism as well as Handel's use of sacred themes for secular purposes. The social prejudices of the society greatly amused Taylor. One such member was greatly upset to learn that the composer also spent his holidays at Westcliff-on-Sea. The person evidently felt it was all right for the conductor to be Negro, but not to sleep in the same neighborhood. Coleridge-Taylor stopped telling too freely from that moment on when or where he would vacation.

There were two festivals Coleridge-Taylor directed
as the regular conductor that are worthy of mention. He
succeeded Sir Henry Wood as director of the Sheffield Music
Festival for three years and conducted the Westmoreland Music Festival for several years also.

Early in 1898 came Coleridge-Taylor's first great opportunity, and he owed it to the generosity of Elgar. Sir
Edward had been asked to write a composition for the pres-
tigious Three Choirs Festival at Gloucester; his answer was
as follows:

> I have received a request from the secretary to
> write a short orchestral thing for the evening concert.
> I am sorry I am too busy to do so. I wish, wish,
> wish you would ask Coleridge-Taylor to do it. He
> still wants recognition, and he is far and away the
> cleverest fellow going amongst the young men. Please
> don't let your committee throw away the chance of do-
> ing a good act. Edward Elgar.

The result was the Ballade in A Minor, a work of im-
mense rhythmical vigor, a barbaric quality, and orchestral
color of great ingenuity. Taylor was a skilled orchestrator
and wrote material for players that fit the character and fingering of the instrument naturally. September 12, 1898,
proved to be the turning point of recognition for Samuel
Coleridge-Taylor.

Commissions for festivals were an integral part of
professional musical success in Victorian England. Music-
making was a way of life for many people through their
choruses and parlor music. But a choral festival in England, or a Welsh competition was the high point not only of
participation by the choristers but recognition of a composer. It meant prestige, publicity and a financial gain. Further, it presented the prospect for more of the same.
Among the many festival commissions that Coleridge-Taylor

enjoyed are:

> The Death of Minnehaha, op. 30, no. 2--the North
> Staffordshire Musical Festival, Hanley
>
> A Solemn Prelude, op. 40--the Three Choirs Festival,
> Worcester
>
> Hiawatha's Departure, op. 30, no. 4--the Royal Choir-
> al Society, London
>
> The Blind Girl of Castel-Cuillé, op. 43--the Leeds
> Musical Festival, Leeds
>
> Meg Blane, op. 48--Sheffield Musical Festival, Shef-
> field
>
> Five Choral Ballads, op. 54--Samuel Coleridge-
> Taylor Choral Society, Washington, D. C.

Coleridge-Taylor's most ambitious sacred work is The
Atonement, a sacred cantata for soloists, chorus and orchestra, op. 53.   This 190-page vocal score was written for the
Three Choirs Festival at Hereford.   This composition occu-
pied most of 1902 and 1903.   Given its first performance on
September 9, 1903, it received a mixed reaction, bordering
on the negative.   The excellent soloists included the famous
soprano, Mme. Albani.   A second performance in the Albert
Hall by the Royal Choral Society was received with greater
success.

The work suffers from an inferior libretto.   In seek-
ing to complete the last phrases of the tragedy, Coleridge-
Taylor remarked that he preferred to set original verses
rather than to select scriptural texts.   He secured a libretto
to his satisfaction from the pen of a member of the Three
Choirs, Mrs. Alice Parsons, wife of a Cheltenham journalist.   The text simply is not outstanding.   In addition,
Coleridge-Taylor may have suggested certain rhythmic pe-
culiarities which resulted in short staccato lines of prose
and inappropriately reflected an imitation of Hiawatha verses.

The public was completely enraptured with the Hiawatha style. It was a barometer of success, but also a compositional hindrance for the composer throughout his life.

The Atonement also violated certain conventions of the time. The last seven words of Christ were sung not by the chorus, but by Christ. The first performance included a duet, distinctly about "love" in character, by Pilate and his wife.

Chapter Two

HIAWATHA: ANALYSIS AND MUSICAL EXAMPLES

Coleridge-Taylor found great inspiration from American literature, in particular the works of Longfellow and Walt Whitman. Early in 1897, when he was but 22, he began work on Hiawatha's Wedding Feast, but it was not finished until the following year. The idea came from Sir Charles Stanford, who had great faith in the composer's ability.

> At first sight it would seem to have been a remarkable choice of subject for musical setting, in spite of the fact that earlier musicians had essayed to deal with the very sections which Coleridge-Taylor was now attempting. The staccato trochaic measure borrowed by Longfellow from the Danish [sic] Kalevala, with its inevitable feminine endings and endless repetitions, promises an effect of monotony which would be fatal if translated into music. But difficulties such as these were a challenge which he would accept with joyous confidence [Sayers, Samuel Coleridge-Taylor (1915), p57].

Longfellow wrote several large poetic works that made up a trilogy about Americana: Evangeline, The Courtship of Miles Standish, and The Song of Hiawatha. Longfellow wanted to weave together Indian traditions. He read the Finnish epic Kalevala, which suggested the rhythm, and may even have reminded him of Indian legend. Longfellow called Hiawatha an Indian "Edda," a word which comes from the

Icelandic and means a great tale about heroes. He was able to draw upon his personal friendship with the Algonquins in Maine to create an imaginative story about Indians, although seen through 19th-century eyes.

The textual source of Coleridge-Taylor's trilogy, Scenes from the Song of Hiawatha, is taken from the 226-page epic, The Song of Hiawatha, by Henry Wadsworth Longfellow. Coleridge-Taylor's Hiawatha's Wedding Feast, the first to be composed, is taken textually from Chapter XI of the poem, and used in its entirety. However, to the end of Chapter XI Coleridge-Taylor added five lines from the ending of Chapter XII, The Son of the Evening Star:

> Such was Hiawatha's Wedding
> Thus the wedding banquet ended,
> And the wedding guests departed,
> Leaving Hiawatha happy,
> With the night and Minnehaha.

The second section of the musical trilogy was The Death of Minnehaha. Here Coleridge-Taylor drew upon Chapter XX, The Famine, which he used with no additions or deletions. Hiawatha's Departure completed the Coleridge-Taylor score. He selected his text from two sections of the poem. This includes the middle of Chapter XXI, The White-Man's Foot, slightly inverted. Instead of "Came the Spring with all its splendor," Taylor changed it to "Spring had come with all its splendor." The poem then continues as written, and proceeds directly into Chapter XXII, Hiawatha's Departure, which is used in its entirety.

The young composer was fascinated by the beauty of the poem and also the curious sounding names such as Pau-Puk-Keewis, Iagoo, Chibiabos, Nokomis.* But more, he

---

*See pp. 69-71.

SCENES FROM THE SONG OF HIAWATHA.

I. HIAWATHA'S WEDDING FEAST.

LONGFELLOW.

S. COLERIDGE-TAYLOR (Op. 30, No. 1).

Coleridge-Taylor—Hiawatha.—Novello.   B   8285.

had a naive manner that found an affinity with the gracious charm of the story, its primitive plot, unaffected expression and unforced idealism.

Coleridge-Taylor was innately shy about, and even contemptuous of publicity and attention. When the finished work was first performed to a wildly enthusiastic audience at the Royal College of Music in 1898, it was necessary for Stanford, its director, to leave the stage and seek out the composer who was hiding offstage. Every London paper devoted considerable space to this unusual work, and without exception acclaimed it an artistic masterpiece. Coleridge-Taylor received only 15 guineas for the outright sale of his opus. Although hundreds of thousands of copies were sold in subsequent years, the 15 guineas remained the composer's total income for his masterpiece, as he had sold the copyright for that first printing and performance.

Popularity and success were so enormous that the composer was soon asked to set the rest of the poem to music, although it was not his initial intention to compose a trilogy. The Death of Minnehaha was commissioned by the North Staffordshire Music Festival in 1899. This oratorio and the subsequent Hiawatha's Departure brought Coleridge-Taylor only £250. He was faced with constant financial problems during his life.

If Hiawatha had in its metrical form presented every prospect of monotony, Minnehaha contained variations suggested by the subjects inherent in the text, including the narrative, the dance, the lovesong and the boasting.

Inevitably, the composer set out to finish the trilogy with Hiawatha's Departure. The earliest drafts were failures. Audiences kept on expecting more and more, but in some respects Coleridge-Taylor had burned out his distinctive personality. It was difficult to maintain the unusual naive and primitive character in all his music.

Auguste J. Jaeger, then music editor at Novello's and a sincere advisor of the young composer, was at first disappointed with Hiawatha's Departure. "This will never do," he said. "The public expects you to progress, to do better work than before; this is your worst." With perseverance the composer perfected his final episode of the Longfellow legend.

It was first performed in conjunction with the two earlier cantatas on March 22, 1900, by the Royal Choral Society in the awesome Albert Hall in London. It was an exhilarating evening for a man of 25: an entire evening devoted to a single work; a choir and orchestra of one thousand and the largest concert hall in the British Empire.

It was considered to be worthy of its companions, although there was some feeling that it was perhaps too long, and that the final chorus needed cutting. From the standpoint of technique it was a great success. The composer continued to astound with his complete command of the art of orchestration and metamorphosis of themes.

Jaeger compared Hiawatha to a symphony, of which the Wedding Feast formed the opening allegro; The Death of Minnehaha, the slow movement; the first portion of The Departure up to the Iagoo scene, the scherzo; and the rest of The Departure, the finale; with the baritone scene, Hiawatha's vision, added as a short fifth movement or intermezzo between the scherzo and finale. The whole work was considered progressing from one movement to the next, but some critics felt that The Departure was too long and needed cutting.

There is actually a fourth part to the Hiawatha canvas. Coleridge-Taylor felt that an overture was needed between The Death of Minnehaha and The Departure. His source of inspiration for the Overture came from the (Fisk) Jubilee Singers, a Negro Choir that had toured England during Coleridge-Taylor's time. He used as his theme the revivalist hymn tune, "Nobody Knows the Trouble I See." He also added archaic-sounding detached chords to give a suggestion of Indian character.

Coleridge-Taylor's music has definite characteristics. He was fond of strong, clear-cut rhythms, which are often repeated. Warmth of melody and abundant color are nearly always features. He memorized the entire poem Hiawatha before attempting to set it to music. He had a fine sense of tone-color and a fascination with words. His own outlook on poetry is intimately reflected in the music he set it to, which seems to bubble with self-expression. He leaned toward solid chords, attractively picturesque changes of key, and vivid dynamic contrasts. He had a fine sense of the effective climax.

I. Hiawatha's Wedding Feast is constructed upon a few simple, but ingratiating melodies. Coleridge-Taylor reflected the rhythmic character of the words and these are clearly manifested in the rhythmic and melodic contours he devised. His great talent lay in not only writing attractive tunes but in making unlimited repetitions in a kaleidescopic range of transformations. These, particularly, utilized colorful harmonizations and orchestration. Consequently, there is no feeling of monotony. Repetitions of themes are subjected to many clever metamorphoses and the result is a

[cont. on p50]

On this and the following four pages are examples of the themes and principal melodies used in <u>Hiawatha</u>.

Fourth Theme

And when all the guests had fin-ish'd,

Old No - ko - mis, brisk and bu - sy,

From an am - ple pouch of ot-ter,

Fill'd the red stone pipes for smok-ing

with to - bac - co from the South-land,

Fifth Theme

Skill'd was he in sports and pas-times,

In the mer - ry dance of snow-shoes ,

In the play of quoits and ball - play;

Skill'd was he in games of haz - ard,

Sixth Theme

He was dress'd in shirt of doe-skin,

White and soft, and fring'd with er - mine,

All in - wrought with beads of wam-pum;

Sixth Theme in G-Flat Major

On his head were plumes of swan's down,

On his heels were tails of fox - es,

feeling of spontaneity, which was to remain an outstanding characteristic of his music.

Nine clearly defined themes are used consistently and each is transformed many times to fit the character of the words. There is also a beautiful tenor solo. The color of the queer-sounding names and the mood of the poem are done with a sense of naturalness and deceptively naive simplicity. The poem has monotonous rhythm and a peculiar style. It was an audacious challenge. The result is very successful and imaginative.

It is related that someone asked Coleridge-Taylor what the opening theme signified. His answer was "Oh! I don't know, I thought it would sound nice." Seldom would the composer give any personal reasons why he composed in a certain way.

The cantata is a continuous descriptive choral narrative which uses several themes in various transformations. It is interrupted once. There is only one solo. It is a ravishingly beautiful tenor song, full of tenderness. "Onaway! Awake, Beloved" has been a great favorite of British tenors for years. Coleridge-Taylor not only wrote a superb, continuous melodic line of noble cantabile tradition, but the harmonic ingenuity and orchestral color are also splendid. Pictorial imagery is one of the composer's outstanding abilities. The aria soars in effective climaxes. No tenor should neglect this magnificent song.

Hiawatha's Wedding Feast is a simple story about the love of two young Indians, Minnehaha and Hiawatha, the preparation for their wedding feast, their guests, celebrations, and good wishes. The imagery is rich and varied in word and music. Various colorful Indian characters are described: Nokomis, the grandmother and her many beautiful preparations;

Pau-Puk-Keewis, the handsome Storm-fool; Chibiabos, the
sweetest of musicians and friend of Hiawatha; Iagoo, a great
boaster and storyteller and perhaps a bit of an exaggerator;
Yenadizze, an idler and gambler; and Shaugadaya, a coward.
A catalog of unusual sounding Indian words is unfolded. Coleridge-Taylor was charmed and intrigued by the
sound of the queer names and he set them to music with
great enthusiasm and imagination. The food at the wedding
feast is described: nahma, maskenozha, pemican, buffalo
marrow, deer, bison, yellow cakes of the mondamin. Indian games and sports are described: pugasaing, koomtassoo.
And some geography: Nagow Wadjoo. But finally "the wedding guests departed, leaving Hiawatha happy, with the night
and Minnehaha. "

II.   The Death of Minnehaha is a remarkable companion to the famous Hiawatha's Wedding Feast. Certain
similarities are inevitable, in particular the rhythmic con-
struction of the subject matter as well as the arrangement
of the text. Meter and style are textually the same in both
settings. Although the Wedding Feast is better known, and
indeed a fine composition, The Death of Minnehaha is a su-
perior work. It manifests the experience of the composer's
rapidly growing lists of opuses, finer craftsmanship and
greater depth of feeling. But there is still the remarkable
feeling of originality and spontaneity. Textually, of course,
there is a great difference. The former is naive in its
storytelling of love and Indian simplicity. The latter cantata
is a heartmoving tragedy.

Coleridge-Taylor again uses short themes which are
developed and treated in a variety of guises. This technique

[cont. on p58]

On this and the following six pages are examples of the themes and principal melodies used in The Death of Minnehaha.

4. Cry of Agony and Despair

5. The Guest--Famine (baritone)

And the foremost said,"Be - hold me! I am

Fam-ine, Buck - a - daw - in !"

6. The Guest--Fever (soprano)

And the other said, "Be - hold me ! I am

Fe - ver, Ah - ko - se - win!"

7. Hiawatha Rushing Into the Forest

Forth in - to the emp - ty for - est

Rushed the mad - den'd Hi - a - wa - tha;

8. Appeal to Gitchie Manito

"Git - che Ma - ni-to, ..., the Might-y,

Git-che Ma-ni-to,... the might- y!"

Cried ... he with his face up-lift - ed,

11. I Will Follow My Husband

And the love-ly Laugh-ing Wa-ter Said, with voice that did not trem-ble, "I will fol - low you, my hus - band!"

12. Soprano Solo

"Hark!" she said, "I hear a rushing, Hear a roar - ing and a rushing. Hear the falls of Min - ne - ha - ha Call - ing to me ... from a dis - tance!"

13. Wahonomin (Death)

"Wa - ho - no - min! Wa - ho-no- min !

Would ... that I had perish'd for you,

Would that I were dead as you are!

14. Soprano Solo

Then he sat down, still and

speech-less, On the bed of Min-ne-

ha- ha , At the feet of Laughing Wa -ter, At those

will - ing feet, that nev - er

more would light-ly run to meet him ,

nev-er more would light-ly fol-low . . .

15. Then They Buried Minnehaha

16. Choral Theme

Then they bu - ried Min - ne - ha - ha

17. Choral Theme

Cov - er'd her with snow-like er - mine

18. Choral Theme

For her soul ... up - on its jour - ney

... to the Is - lands of the Bless-ed ...

19. Farewell to Minnehaha

"Fare - well!",said he,"Min-ne -ha- ha! Fare-

well, O my Laughing Wa- ter!... All my heart is

is particularly successful with the composer. It is not necessarily an extended theme and variation technique. Instead,
it is a short embryonic device which is used in a variety of
transformations.

It is possible to identify many themes with descriptive titles. Each has a role to play in depicting the impending tragedy. In some respects, one can think of this
in the same manner as a Wagnerian leitmotif.

The last chorus describes the burial of Minnehaha
and the despairing sorrow of her husband, Hiawatha. It was

a difficult challenge for the composer, but it reaches a high degree of heart-rending pathos and sheer unpretentious musical beauty.

The opening 50 measures use descriptive motifs (themes 1-4). An atmosphere of tragedy is quickly created. The chorus enters and repeats these themes, divided into four sections, each connected by short orchestral interludes. This introductory section takes 8-1/2 pages of vocal score.

With the entry of the Ghosts, Famine and Fever, the music changes in character. Famine is sung by the baritone soloist (theme 5) and fever by the soprano soloist (theme 6). The composer continues with 16-1/2 pages in the vocal score of highly descriptive music. A series of tragic events are unfolded, including Minnehaha's fear of her doom--"And the lovely Minnehaha shuddered as they look down upon her, shuddered at the words they uttered, lay down on her bed in silence"; Hiawatha's rushing into the forest to cry to Gitche Manito (themes 7, 8, 9); the silence as the voices sing of Hiawatha's cry of desolation--"there came no answer than the echo of his crying" (theme 10); the ray of hope through the reminiscences when Hiawatha rowed in the "melancholy forest" through which he had brought his young wife "in that ne'er forgotten summer"; and concluding with the fervent last desperate hope of Minnehaha--"I will follow you, my husband" (theme 11).

The next section of 14 pages is vividly full of highly descriptive and deeply felt emotions and includes the shriek and cry of Minnehaha to her husband. But the brave of the bravest cannot return in time, for Hiawatha finds Minnehaha his beloved only in death.

Coleridge-Taylor makes effective use of many fermatas (holds) in the opening soprano solo, with women's chorus, "Hush, I hear a rushing" (theme 12). These short phrases followed by fermatas, are suggestive of the ferverish gasping for breath and agonizing suspense. Finally, Minnehaha's last cry with terror, "Oh, the eyes of Pauguk [Death] glare upon me in the darkness; I can feel his icy fingers clasping mine amid the darkness," is followed by a scream of help, "Hiawatha!" Here a descending diminished seventh from A-flat is echoed by oboe and clarinet, and afterwards by full orchestra.

Hiawatha has hurried home "empty handed, empty hearted," and hears Nokomis weep over Minnehaha (theme 13). This is sung by baritone solo, followed by unaccompanied chorus, "as if the Chief's braves and their squaws joined in the lamentation" (Musical Times, Dec. 1, 1899, p814). Hiawatha rushes into the wigwam to see his lovely bride "lying dead and cold before him" and in a swoon he laments "such a cry of anguish that the very stars in heaven shook and trembled!" (theme 14).

The concluding 13-page movement is a very impressive funeral march (Moderato, quasi una marcia funebre). The voices sing largely in unison, the orchestration is full, deep and sombre. The choral melodic line is simple but emotionally charged (theme 14). Two secondary themes (16 and 17) are also used with great ingenuity. In particular, Coleridge-Taylor repeats a sad phrase of four notes (theme 16) on different degrees of the scale, against unusual, changing harmonies. The orchestration throbs with the beat of brass and drums. Throughout, the text is richly descriptive and emotionally charged.

The last solo, for baritone (Larghetto lamentoso, come la prima) is a pathetic farewell to the dead Minnehaha (theme 19). It is a heart overflowing with grief and pity.

The chorus, with many vivid variations, repeats the baritone solo, leading to one of the composer's outstanding climaxes, "To the land of the hereafter" (theme 20). This climax is unaccompanied until "hereafter," when the orchestra reenters with a dominant minor ninth chord, with the sopranos singing a bright major thirteenth. Ten measures of effective orchestral writings bring the Death of Minnehaha to a close.

III. Hiawatha's Departure was the inevitable conclusion to a musical work of imagination and innate charm. It was also the continuation of a technique and style that was highly personal. Although Coleridge-Taylor had studied and was evidently a good student in contrapuntal technique, he was never to manifest this to any great extent in his compositions. The language was essentially harmonic. Not chromatic harmony or the florid modulatory style of Wagner, but an interesting and personal style. The composer was fond of beautiful melody with solid harmonic support, triads, seventh chords, fluctuations between major and minor tonalities, subtle key changes and attractive rhythmic patterns.

The concluding cantata begins with a 30-measure orchestral introduction, bright and catchy, leading into an attractive soprano solo (theme 1), "Spring had come with all its splendour." It is accompanied by a sprightly melodic figure (theme 2). The modulations in the solo go from the original D major to G major, A major, F-sharp minor, a return to D major, a section in D minor and a final return to D major. All these keys are of course related: G is the sub-dominant and A the dominant of D major, F-sharp is the relative minor of A major and D minor is the parallel of D major. [cont. on p66]

1. Soprano Solo

Spring had come with all its splen-dour, All its

birds and all its blossoms, All its flow'rs and

leaves and grass-es, all its flow'rs ...

and leaves and grass-es ....

2. Accompanimental Figure

3. Theme Unison Melody

From his wan-d'rings far to east- ward, From the

re - gions of the morn-ing, From the shin - ing

land of Wa - bun, Home- ward now re-turn'd I -

a - goo,

4. Choral Theme

At each o - ther look'd the war- ri- ors,

Look'd the wo - men at each o - ther

Smil'd, and said, "It can-not be so!

5. Wedding Feast Theme

6. Bass Solo

" True is all I - a - goo tells us; I have

seen it in a vi - sion, Seen the

great can-oe with pin-ions, ...

7. By the Shore of Gitche Gumee

By the shore.. of Git-che Gu - mee

By the shore of Git - che Gu - mee

8. Choral Theme

9. Soprano Solo

10. Baritone Solo

11. Joyous Theme

Then the generous Hi - a

wa - tha led the strangers to his wig - wam,

Seat-ed the mon skins of bis-on,... Seat-ed them on

skins of er - mine,

12. Wedding Feast Theme

Still the guests ... of Hi - a - wa - tha

13. Wedding Feast Theme

From his place rose Hi - a - wa - tha

Repetition of the Wail Theme

sf

morendo

p

14. Final Chorus of Farewell

A change of time signature is effected from duple to
triple meter in the choral section "From his wanderings far
to eastward" (theme 3). It leads into a declamatory section
between tenor solo and chorus, quasi recitativo and leggiero.
Iagoo effectively depicts the arrival of white men in "a
canoe with wings." But the warriors and their women only
looked at each other, laughed and said "Kaw! We don't

believe it" (theme 4). The first time, the tenor's quasi recitativo line is in F major and the chorus answers in G major. This is repeated. However, the third time it modulates from A minor to E minor. But in one final descriptive cry, the tenor sings in G major, and the chorus answers
in A major, modulating to E minor when "only Hiawatha
laughed not. "

Hiawatha had the vision to know that the arrival of
the white man meant an end to the Indians' world. A two-
measure bridge (theme 5) leads into an emotional 140-mea-
sure solo for baritone (theme 6), again quasi recitativo, but
also ben declamado. It is quite noticeable that the composer
frequently employs sung dialogue (recitativo) in the third cantata, in order to effectively capture the narrative character
of the story.

After a 24-measure orchestral interlude, allegro vivace, the chorus sings a 51-measure section describing the
beauties of nature, which is then repeated with a different
text. The musical ideas are developed. One is harmonical-
ly energetic (theme 7) and the second is treated imitatively
(theme 8).

A lovely soprano solo with chorus follows (theme 9).
The Indians see a strange sight and wonder what it is. "It
is neither goose nor diver, neither pelican nor heron, o'er
the water floating. " It is the Paleface and the Black Robe
Chief with the cross upon his bosom. They are greeted with
great dignity by Hiawatha in a baritone solo, "Beautiful is
the sun, o strangers" (theme 10). "The Black Robe Chief
made answer ... Peace be with you. " This is followed by
a joyful chorus with melody (theme 11) treated in a variety
of coloristic guises.

The white priest tells the Indians about Mary, her Son and Saviour. Indian chiefs listen politely and promise to consider this new message. Sunset descends and the guests of Hiawatha slumber. Coleridge-Taylor recapitulates two important themes from the first cantata, Hiawatha's Wedding Feast (themes 12 and 13). It is a stroke of genius that he could relate the impending tragedy with the metamorphosis of these earlier themes. This is of course one of the distinctive features of the composer.

But Hiawatha's time has come. Taylor builds the music from this point on to one effective climax after another. Hiawatha bids an impassioned farewell, "I am going, o my people, on a long and distant journey: many moons and many moons will have come and will have vanish'd, ere I come to see you."

After this dramatic episode, the composer indicates a possible cut in the score. It will be recalled that he was criticized for making the score too long. He indicated this possible cut: "If desired, the section between 73A and 82 may be omitted in performance, in which case these 10 bars in small type must be used." It is a lovely section of 130 measures, quite pathetic in its emotion. It should not be cut.

But ultimately Hiawatha turns, waves farewell and sets sail into the fiery sunset. The composer weaves a variety of short themes into the tapestry of which the predominant is the one he used in the opening of Hiawatha's Wedding Feast (theme 12).

The three-part cantata ends with another musical climax. Coleridge-Taylor was able to find something new to say each time and somehow avoid an anti-climax. It is an impassioned chorus of farewell to Hiawatha the Beloved (theme 14).

Hiawatha / 69

Translation and Pronunciation of the Indian Words
In "Scenes from the Song of Hiawatha"*

AHKOSE'WIN   Äh-kŏ-sē-win (fever)

AH'MO   Äh-mō (the stinging fly)

ANNEMEE'KEE   Än-ne-mē-kē (the thunder)

BUCKADAW'IN   Buck-ä-dāw-in (famine)

CA'LUMET   Cä-lū-met (a pipe; used as a symbol
                  of peace, and as evidence to strangers
                  that they are welcome)

CHIBIA'BOS   Chĕ-bi-ä-bos [soft ch] (a musician;
                  friend of Hiawatha, Ruler in the Land
                  of Spirits)

DACO'TAHS   Dä-cŏ-tähs (a race of Indians, includ-
[or Dakotas]   ing many tribes dwelling mostly west
                  of the Mississippi; also in part, called
                  Sioux)

GITCHE GU'MEE   Git-che Gū-mē (the Big Sea-Water,
                  Lake Superior)

GITCHE MAN'ITO   Git-che Mä-ni-tō (the Great Spirit,
                  the Master of Life)

HIAWA'THA   Hī-ä-wä-thä (the prophet, the teach-
                  er; son of Mudjekeewis, the West
                  Wind, and Wenonah)

IA'GOO   I-ä-goo (a great boaster and story-
                  teller)

JOSS'AKEED   Jos-sä-kēd (a prophet)

KAW   Kāw (no)

KEEWAY'DIN   Kē-wā-din (the Northwest Wind, the
                  home wind.

KOOMTASSOO'   Koom-tä-soo (the game of plum
                  stones)

MAHNAHBE'ZEE   Mä-nä-be-zē (the swan)

MAHNG   Mäng (the loon, the northern diver
                  [Urinator imber]; a web-footed bird,

*ā = flaw, ä = fäther, a = am, ā = āle, e = end, ē = ēve,
ī = hīde, i = ill, ŏ = cŏw, o = odd, ō = ōld, ū = rūde,
u = up.

notable for its ability in diving and
swimming under water)

MASKENOZHA	Măs-ke-nō-ză (the pike)
ME'DA	Mēdă (a medicine man)
MINJEKAH'WUN	Min-je-kă-wūn (Hiawatha's mittens)
MINNEHA'HA	Min-nĕ-hă-hă (Laughing Water, the wife of Hiawatha)
MOND'AMIN	Mōn-dă-min (Indian Corn)
MUSHKODA'SA	Mūsh-kō-dă-să (the grouse)
NA'GOW WUDJOO'	Nă-gō Wu-joo (the sand dunes of Lake Superior)
NAH'MA	Nă-mă (the sturgeon)
NOKO'MIS	Nō-kō-mis (grandmother of Hiawatha, mother of Wenonah)
OME'ME	Ō-mē-mē (the pigeon)
ONAWAY'	O-nă-wā (awake)
OPECHEE'	Ō-pē-chē (the robin)
OSSE'O	Os-sē-yō (Son of the Evening Star)
OWAIS'-SA	Ō-wās-să (the blue-bird; a small song bird [Sialia sialis], common in North America; it is related to the European robin)
PAH-PUK-KEE'NA	Pă-pūk-kē-nă (the grasshopper)
PAUGUK	Pŏw-gūk (death)
PAH-PUK-KEE'WIS	Pŏw-pūk-kē-wis (the handsome Yena-dizze, the Storm-Fool)
PEM'ICAN	Pem-i-kan (meat of the deer or buf-falo, dried and pounded)
PONE'MAH	Pō-nē-măh (hereafter)
PUGASAING	Poog-ă-sā-ing (the game of bowl and counters)
SHADA	Shă-dă (the pelican)
SHAUGODAYA	Shou-gō-dă-yă (a coward)
SHIN'GEBIS	Shin-ge-bis (the diver or grebe, a swimming bird of the genus Colymbus)

SHUH'-SHUH'-GAH	Shū-shū-gäh (the blue heron)
UGH	Ūgh (yes)
WABE'NO	Wä-bē-nō (a magician; a juggler)
WA'BUN	Wä-būn (the East Wind)
WAHONO'MIN	Wäh-hō-nō-min (a cry of lamentation)
WAW-BE-WA'WA	Wä-bē-wä-wä (the white goose)
WAYWAS'SIMO	Wā-wäs-si-mō (the lightening)
WIGWAM	Wig-wäm (Indian tent)
YENADIZ'ZE	Ye-nä-diz-zā (an idler and gambler, an Indian dandy)

Chapter Three

AMERICA AND SUCCESS

Three glorious, happy visits were made by Coleridge-
Taylor to the United States in 1904, 1906 and 1910. The
impetus for the first visit came from the Samuel Coleridge-
Taylor Society of Washington, D. C. Organized in 1901, its
purpose was to produce the works of the black composer.
It enjoyed a long and successful existence. The society was
without precedent in musical history in that it consisted entirely of members of the Negro race and was trained by a
Negro conductor. Although the Fisk Jubilee Singers was in
existence for over 25 years before the Washington Society,
the 200-member Washington Society was the first to devote
itself to the study and performance of the great choral mas-
terpieces of the world.

Their invitation to the composer was offered on December 17, 1901, but circumstances prevented him from ac-
cepting it until 1904. American Negroes looked upon
Coleridge-Taylor as an outstanding example to their race:
a man of intellect, talent and success. He became a household word and an inspiration in many American Negro homes
and model of one who could overcome racial and prejudicial
difficulties.

Most of Coleridge-Taylor's correspondence with the
Washington, D. C. , society was with its treasurer, Mr.

Andrew F. Hilyer. The society had some trepidation that
the visiting composer might experience racial prejudice and
difficulties, and might become the target of insults. Coleridge-Taylor had no such fears. In a letter to Mr. Hilyer
dated September 14, 1904, the composer offered the following positive feelings:

> I can assure you that no one will be able to stop me
> from paying you my long deferred visit. As for pre-
> judice, I am well prepared for it. Surely that which
> you and many others have lived in for so many years
> will not quite kill me.
>
> I don't think anything else would have induced me
> to visit America, excepting the fact of an established
> society of coloured singers; it is for that, first and
> foremost, that I am coming, and all other engage-
> ments are secondary.
>
> I am a great believer in my race, and I never
> lose an opportunity of letting my white friends here
> know it. Please don't make any arrangements to
> wrap me in cotton-wool. I am not that kind of per-
> son at all. I do a great deal of adjudicating in Wales
> among a very rough class of people; most adjudicators
> have had bad eggs and boots thrown at them by the
> people, but fortunately nothing of the kind has ever
> happened to me yet. I mention this so that you may
> know my life is not spent entirely in drawing-rooms
> and concert halls, but among some of the roughest
> people in the world, who tell you what they think very
> plainly. Yet I have four more engagements among
> them for next January.

It was also in the year 1904 that Coleridge-Taylor
read DuBois's The Souls of Black Folk. It was a revelation
to him, leading him to use Negro folk music from Africa
and the United States. Because of his early success, in
particular with Hiawatha, Coleridge-Taylor was admired by
the black community in the United States as a leader and indeed as the prototype for a renaissance of black culture.

William Edward Burghardt DuBois (1868-1963) was
one of the best versed, most articulate, and most militant

leaders of black Americans. Although DuBois enjoyed a long
and productive career, he is best remembered for his collection of essays entitled The Souls of Black Folk. His educa-
tional background included Fisk University, a Ph.D. from
Harvard in 1895, and further studies in Berlin. An important goal in his career was to scientifically research studies
on the Negro of which the first, The Philadelphia Negro: A
Social Study, appeared in 1899. Subsequently he investigated
the areas of the Negro church, schools and occupations.

In 1905, DuBois organized the Niagara movement, a
group of militant young black intellectuals. The group, together with several other groups, both black and white,
joined forces in 1909 to become the National Association for
the Advancement of Colored People, which is still a vital
movement.

Early in 1904 Coleridge-Taylor told Sayers that he
had just finished "the greatest book I have ever read." The
book, Souls of Black Folk, was sent to him by Andrew F.
Hilyer. In a letter of January 3, 1904, Taylor answered:

Dear Mr. Hilyer,

This is only a line to thank you over and over
again for so kindly sending me the book by Mr.
DuBois. It is about the finest book I have ever read
by a coloured man, and one of the best by any author, white and black.
Expect another letter from me shortly. For the
moment I have many other letters to write, so I
know you will forgive so short an epistle.
With every good wish for the New Year to you
and Mrs. Hilyer,

Believe me
Yours sincerely
S. Coleridge-Taylor

Opposite page: The Coleridge-Taylor Choral Society, Washington, D.C.

In the preface to The Souls of Black Folk, DuBois
wrote, "I have sought to sketch in vague, uncertain outline,
the spiritual world in which ten thousand Americans live and
strive. " The last essay is entitled "Of the Sorrow Songs"
and is a discussion of Negro folksongs. It made a profound
impression upon Coleridge-Taylor and is reprinted here.

"Of the Sorrow Songs"
The Souls of Black Folk (1903)

"They that walked in darkness sang songs in the
olden days---Sorrow Songs---for they were weary at
heart. And so before each thought that I have written
in this book I have set a phrase, a haunting echo of
these weird old songs in which the soul of the black
slave spoke to men. Ever since I was a child these
songs have stirred me strangely. They came out of
the South unknown to me, one by one, and yet at once
I knew them as of me and of mine. Then in after
years when I came to Nashville I saw the great temple
builded of these songs towering over the pale city. To
me Jubilee Hall seemed ever made of the songs themselves, and its bricks were red with the blood and dust
of toil. Out of them rose for me morning, noon, and
night, bursts of wonderful melody, full of the voices
of my brothers and sisters, full of the voices of the
past.

"Little of beauty has America given the world save
the rude grandeur God himself stamped on her bosom;
the human spirit in this new world has expressed itself in vigor and ingenuity rather than in beauty. And
so by fateful chance the Negro folk song--the rhythmic
cry of the slave--stands to-day not simply as the sole

American music, but as the most beautiful expression
of human experience, born this side [of] the seas. It
has been neglected, it has been, and is, half despised,
and above all it has been persistently mistaken and misunderstood; but notwithstanding, it still remains as the
singular spiritual heritage of the nation and the greatest
gift of the Negro people.

"Away back in the thirties the melody of these
slave songs stirred the nation, but the songs were soon
half forgotten. Some, like 'Near the lake where drooped
the willow,' passed into current airs and their source
was forgotten; others were caricatured on the 'minstrel'
stage and their memory died away. Then in war-time
came the singular Port-Royal experiment after the capture of Hilton Head, and perhaps for the first time the
North met the Southern slave face to face and heart to
heart with no third witness. The Sea Islands of the
Carolinas, where they met, were filled with a black
folk of primitive type, touched and moulded less by the
world about them than any others outside the Black
Belt. Their appearance was uncouth, their language
funny, but their hearts were human and their singing
stirred men with a mighty power. Thomas Wentworth
Higginson hastened to tell of these songs, and Miss
McKim and others urged upon the world their rare
beauty. But the world listened only half credulously
until the Fisk Jubilee Singers sang the slave songs so
deeply into the world's heart that it can never wholly
forget them again.

"There was once a blacksmith's son born in Cadiz,
New York, who in the changes of time taught school
in Ohio and helped defend Cincinnati from Kirby Smith.

Then he fought at Chancellorsville and Gettysburg and finally served in the Freedman's Bureau at Nashville. Here he formed a Sunday-school class of black children in 1866, and sang with them and taught them to sing. And then they taught him to sing, and when once the glory of the Jubilee songs passed into the soul of George L. White, he knew his life-work was to let those Negroes sing to the world as they had sung to him. So in 1871 the pilgrimage of the Fisk Jubilee Singers began. North to Cincinnati they rode--four half-clothed black boys and five girl-women,--led by a man with a cause and a purpose. They stopped at Wilberforce, the oldest Negro school, where a black bishop blessed them. Then they went, fighting cold and starvation, shut out of hotels, and cheerfully sneered at, ever northward; and ever the magic of their song kept thrilling hearts, while a burst of applause in the Congregational Council at Oberlin revealed them to the world. They came to New York and Henry Ward Beecher dared to welcome them, even though the metropolitan dailies sneered at his 'Nigger Minstrels.' So their songs conquered till they sang across the land and across the sea, before Queen and Kaiser, in Scotland and Ireland, Holland and Switzerland. Seven years they sang, and brought back a hundred and fifty thousand dollars to found Fisk University.

"Since their day they have been imitated--sometimes well, by the singers of Hampton and Atlanta, sometimes ill, by straggling quartettes. Caricature has sought again to spoil the quaint beauty of the music, and has filled the air with many debased melodies which vulgar ears scarce know from the real. But the true Negro folk-song still lives in the hearts of those who have heard them truly sung and in the hearts of the Negro people.

"What are these songs, and what do they mean? I know little of music and can say nothing in technical phrase, but I know something of men, and knowing them, I know that these songs are the articulate message of the slave to the world. They tell us in these eager days that life was joyous to the black slave, careless and happy. I can easily believe this of some, of many. But not all the past South, though it rose from the dead, can gainsay the heart-touching witness of these songs. They are the music of an unhappy people, of the children of disappointment; they tell of death and sufferings and unvoiced longing toward a truer world, of misty wanderings and hidden ways.

"The songs are indeed the siftings of centuries; the music is far more ancient than the words, and in it we can trace here and there signs of development. My grandfather's grandmother was seized by an evil Dutch trader two centuries ago; and coming to the valleys of the Hudson and Housatonic, black, little, and lithe, she shivered and shrank in the harsh north winds, looked longingly at the hills, and often crooned a heathen melody to the child between her knees, thus:

Do   ba-na co- ba, ge-ne   me   ge-ne   me!

Do   ba-na co-ba , ge-ne   me,   ge-ne   me!

Ben   d'nu-li , nu -li , nu-li ,nu- li, ben   d' le

"The child sang it to his children and they to their children's children, and so two hundred years it has travelled down to us and we sing it to our children, knowing as little as our fathers what its words may mean, but knowing well the meaning of its music.

"This was primitive African music; it may be seen in larger form in the strange chant which heralds 'The Coming of John':

You may bury me in the East,
You may bury me in the West,
But I'll hear the trumpet sound in the morning.

--the voice of exile.

"Ten master songs, more or less, one may pluck from this forest of melody--songs of undoubted Negro origin and wide popular currency, and songs peculiarly characteristic of the slave. One of these I have just mentioned. Another whose strains begin this book is 'Nobody knows the trouble I've seen.' When struck with sudden poverty, the United States refused to fulfill its promises of land to the freedmen, a brigadier-general went down to the Sea Islands to carry the news. An old woman on the outskirts of the throng began singing this song; all the mass joined with her, swaying. And the soldier wept.

"The third song is the cradle-song of death which all men know, --'Swing low, sweet chariot,'--whose bars begin the life story of 'Alexander Crummel.' Then there is the song of many waters, 'Roll, Jordan, roll,' a mighty chorus with minor cadences. There were many songs of the fugitive like that which opens 'The Wings of Atlanta,' and the more familiar 'Been a-listening.' The seventh is the song of the End and the

Beginning--'My Lord, what a mourning [sic]! when the
stars begin to fall'; a strain of this is placed before
'The Dawn of Freedom. ' The song of groping--'My
way's cloudy'--begins 'The Meaning of Progress'; the
ninth is the song of this chapter--'Wrestlin' Jacob, the
day is a-breaking, '--a paean of hopeful strife. The
last master song is the song of songs--'Steal away'--
sprung from 'The Faith of the Fathers. '

"There are many others of the Negro folk-songs
as striking and characteristic as these ... and others
I am sure could easily make a selection on more scientific principles. There are, too, songs that seem to
be a step removed from the more primitive types:
There is the maze-like medley, 'Bright sparkles, ' one
phrase of which heads 'The Black Belt'; the Easter
carol, 'Dust, dust and ashes'; the dirge, 'My mother's
took her flight and gone home'; and that burst of melody hovering over 'The Passing of the First-Born'--
'I hope my mother will be there in that beautiful world
on high. '

"These represent a third step in the development
of the slave song, of which 'You may bury me in the
East' is the first, and songs like 'March on' ... and
'Steal away' are the second. The first is African music, the second Afro-American, while the third is a
blending of Negro music with the music heard in the
foster land. The result is still distinctively Negro and
the method of blending original, but the elements are
both Negro and Caucasian. One might go further and
find a fourth step in this development, where the songs
of white America have been distinctively influenced by
the slave songs or have incorporated whole phrases of

Negro melody, as 'Swanee River' and 'Old Black Joe.'
Side by side, too, with the growth has gone the debase-
ments and imitations--the Negro 'minstrel' songs,
many of the 'gospel' hymns, and some of the contemporary 'coon' songs, --a mass of music in which the
novice may easily lose himself and never find the real
Negro melodies.

'In these songs, as I have said, the slave spoke
to the world. Such a message is naturally veiled and
half articulate. Words and music have lost each other
and new and cant phrases of a dimly understood theology
have displaced the older sentiment. Once in a while
we catch a strange word of an unknown tongue, as the
'Mighty Myo,' which figures as a river of death; more
often slight words or mere doggerel are joined to music of singular sweetness. Purely secular songs are
few in number, partly because many of them were
turned into hymns by a change of words, partly because the frolics were seldom heard by the stranger,
and the music less often caught. Of nearly all the
songs, however, the music is distinctly sorrowful.
The ten master songs I have mentioned tell in word
and music of trouble and exile, of strife and hidings;
they grope toward some unseen power and sigh for
rest in the End.

"The words that are left to us are not without interest, and, cleared of evident dross, they conceal
much of real poetry and meaning beneath conventional
theology and unmeaning rhapsody. Like all primitive
folk, the slave stood near to Nature's heart. Life
was a 'rough and rolling sea' like the brown Atlantic
of the Sea Islands; the 'Wilderness' was the home of

God, and the 'lonesome valley' led to the way of life.
'Winter'll soon be over,' was the picture of life and
death to a tropical imagination. The sudden wild thun-
derstorms of the South awed and impressed the Negroes,--at times the rumbling seemed to them 'mourn-
ful,' at times imperious:

> 'My Lord calls me,
> He calls me by the thunder,
> The trumpet sounds it in my soul.'

"The monotonous toil and exposure is painted in
many words. One sees the ploughmen in the hot, moist
furrow, singing:

> 'Dere's no rain to wet you,
> Dere's no sun to burn you,
> Oh, push along, believer,
> I want to go home.'

"The bowed and bent old man cries, with thrice-
repeated wail:

> 'O Lord, keep me from sinking down,'

and he rebukes the devil of doubt who can whisper:

> 'Jesus is dead and God's gone away.'

Yet the soul-hunger is there, the restlessness of the
savage, the wail of the wanderer, and the plaint is put
in one little phrase:

My soul wants some-thing that's new, that's new

"Over the inner thoughts of the slaves and their
relations one with another the shadow of fear ever
hung, so that we get but glimpses here and there, and
also with them, eloquent omissions and silences.
Mother and child are sung, but seldom father; fugitive

and weary wanderer call for pity and affection, but
there is little of wooing and wedding; the rocks and the
mountains are well known, but home is unknown.
Strange blending of love and helplessness sighs through
the refrain:

> 'Yonder's my ole mudder,
> Been waggin' at de hill so long;
> 'Bout time she cross over,
> Git home bime-by. '

Elsewhere comes the cry of the 'motherless' and the
'Farewell, farewell, my only child. '

"Love-songs are scarce and fall into two cate-
gories--the frivolous and light, and the sad. Of deep
successful love there is ominous silence, and in one of
the oldest of these songs there is a depth of history
and meaning:

Poor Ro-sy, poor gal, Poor Ro-sy, poor gal;
Ro-sy break my poor heart, Heav'n shall-a be my home.

A black woman said of the song, 'It can't be sung without a full heart and a troubled sperrit. ' The same
voice sings here that sings in the German folk-song:

> 'Jetz Geh i' an's brunele, trink'aber net. '*

"Of death the Negro showed little fear, but talked
of it familiarly and even fondly as simply a crossing
of the waters, perhaps--who knows?--back to his ancient forests again. Later days transfigured his

---

*"Now I go to the fountain, but I don't drink. "

fatalism, and amid the dust and dirt the toiler sang:
'Dust, dust and ashes, fly over my grave,
But the Lord shall bear my spirit home. '
"The things evidently borrowed from surrounding
world undergo characteristic change when they enter
the mouth of the slave. Especially is this true of Bible
phrases. 'Weep, O captive daughter of Zion, ' is
quaintly turned into 'Zion, weep-a-low, ' and the wheels
of Ezekial are turned every way in the mystic dreaming of the slave till he says:
'There's a little wheel a-turnin' in-a-my heart. '
"As in olden time, the words of these hymns were
improvised by some leading minstrel of the religious
band. The circumstances of the gathering, however,
the rhythm of the songs, and the limitations of allow-
able thought, confined the poetry for the most part to
single or double lines, and they seldom are expanded
to quatrains or longer tales, although there are some
few examples of sustained efforts, chiefly paraphrases
of the Bible. Three short series of verses have always attracted me, --the one that heads this chapter, *
of one line of which Thomas Wentworth Higginson has
fittingly said, 'Never, it seems to me, since man first
lived and suffered was his infinite longing for peace
uttered more plaintively. ' The second and third are
descriptions of the Last Judgment, --the one a late im-
provisation, with some traces of outside influence:

*'I walk through the churchyard/ To lay this body down;/
I know moon-rise, I know star-rise;/ I walk in the moon-
light, I walk in the starlight;/ I'll lie in the grave and
stretch out my arms, / I'll go to judgment in the evening of
the day, / And my soul and thy soul shall meet that day, /
When I lay this body down. "

> 'Oh, the stars in the elements are falling,
> And the moon drips away into blood,
> And the ransomed of the Lord are returning unto
>   God,
> Blessed be the name of the Lord. '

And the other earlier and homelier picture from the
low coast lands:

> 'Michael, haul the boat ashore,
> Then you'll hear the horn they blow,
> Then you'll hear the trumpet sound,
> Trumpet sound the world around
> Trumpet sound for rich and poor,
> Trumpet sound the Jubilee,
> Trumpet sound for you and me. '

"Through all the sorrow of the Sorrow Songs there
breathes a hope--a faith in the ultimate justice of things.
The minor cadences of despair change often to triumph
and calm confidence. Sometimes it is faith in life,
sometimes a faith in death, sometimes assurance of
boundless justice in some fair world beyond. But
whichever it is, the meaning is always clear: that
sometime, somewhere, men will judge men by their
souls and not by their skins. Is such a hope justified?
Do the Sorrow Songs sing true?

"The silently growing assumption of this age is that
the probation of races is past, and that the backward
races of to-day are of proven inefficiency and not
worth the saving. Such an assumption is the arrogance
of peoples irreverent toward Time and ignorant of the
deeds of men. A thousand years ago such an assumption, easily possible, would have made it difficult for
the Teuton to prove his right to life. Two thousand
years ago such dogmatism, readily welcome, would
have scouted [scoffed] the idea of blond races ever
leading civilization. So woefully unorganized is

sociological knowledge that the meaning of progress, the meaning of 'swift' and 'slow' in human doing, and the limits of human perfectability, are veiled, un-answered sphinxes on the shores of science. Why should Aeschylus have sung two thousand years before Shakespeare was born? Why has civilization flourished in Europe, and flickered, flamed, and died in Africa? So long as the world stands meekly dumb before such questions, shall this nation proclaim its ignorance and unhallowed prejudices by denying freedom of oppor-tunity to those who brought in the Sorrow Songs to the Seats of the Mighty?

"Your country? How came it yours? Before the Pilgrims landed we were here. Here we have brought our three gifts and mingled them with yours: a gift of story and song--soft, stirring melody in an ill-har-monized and unmelodious land; the gift of sweat and brawn to beat back the wilderness, conquer the soil, and lay the foundations of this vast economic empire two hundred years earlier than your weak hands could have done it; the third, a gift of the Spirit. Around as the history of the land has centred for thrice a hun-dred years; out of the nation's heart we have called all that was best to throttle and subdue all that was worst; fire and blood, prayer and sacrifice, have billowed over this people, and they have found peace only in the altars of the God of Right. Nor has our gift of the Spirit been merely passive. Actively we have woven ourselves with the very warp and woof of this nation, --we fought their battles, shared their sor-row, mingled our blood with theirs, and generation after generation have pleaded with a headstrong, careless people to despise not Justice, Mercy, and Truth, lest the nation be smitten with a curse. Our song, our toil, our cheer, and warning have been given to this nation in blood-brotherhood. Are not these gifts worth the giving? Is not this work and striving? Would America have been America without her Negro people?

"Even so is the hope that sang in the songs of my fathers well sung. If somewhere in this whirl and chaos of things there dwells Eternal Good, pitiful yet masterful, then anon in His good time America shall rend the Veil and the prisoned shall go free. Free, free as the sunshine trickling down the morning into these high windows of mine, free as yonder fresh young voices welling up to me from the caverns of brick and mortar below--swelling with song, instinct with life, tremulous treble and darkening bass, my children, my little children, are singing to the sunshine, and thus they sing:

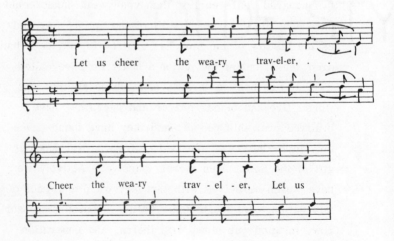

Let us cheer the wea-ry trav-el-er, . .

Cheer the wea-ry trav - el - er, Let us

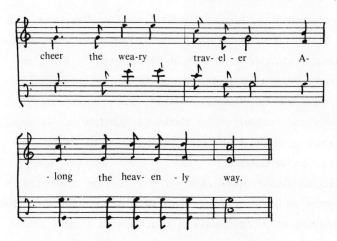

cheer   the wea-ry   trav- el - er   A-

- long   the heav- en - ly   way.

And the traveler girds himself, and sets his face toward the Morning, and goes his way. "

*   *   *   *   *

Beckoned by stirring writings and new friends found
in the United States, the composer finally accepted the stand-
ing invitation from the Samuel Coleridge-Taylor Society of
Washington, D.C. and on October 25, 1904, left for Boston
and his first American tour. The tour included visits to
Washington, New York, Chicago, Baltimore and Boston. Intimate and lasting friendships were developed not only among
his own people, but with members of the white community.
The climax of the tour was a Coleridge-Taylor Festival:
two concerts in Washington's Constitution Hall and one in
Baltimore. The audiences were always mixed wherever he
performed. He paid visits to Howard University, the Washington Normal School and the Armstrong Training School.
A baton made from cedar on the estate of the Negro leader
Frederick Douglass was given to him by the pupils of the M
Street High School for Girls. Coleridge-Taylor was also

deeply touched and honored to be invited by President Theodore Roosevelt to the White House. For some time after his return home from Boston on December 13, 1904, he seriously thought about emigrating to the United States.

Booker T. Washington (1856-1915), American Negro educator and founder of the Tuskegee Institute in Alabama, was another of the four great black American friends and inspirations to Coleridge-Taylor. After the Civil War, Washington first worked in a salt furnace and afterward in a coal mine in Malden, West Virginia. After many difficulties he obtained some rudiments of education in a night school and was finally able to enter the Hampton Institute where he studied from 1872-1875. Later he became an instructor at Hampton.

His most significant contribution was the founding of Tuskegee. Early in 1881 he was selected by General Samuel C. Armstrong, principal of Hampton, on the application of citizens of Tuskegee, Alabama, to start a Negro normal school. Washington opened the school with himself as the only instructor, an enrollment of 30 students and an old church and shanty as his only buildings. His primary concern was to give Negroes a practical education in industry and trade, leading to economic independence.

Although Coleridge-Taylor greatly enjoyed his visit with Booker Washington during his American tour of 1904, he disagreed with the American's idea of limiting Negro instruction to the utilitarian and abandoning the creative and artistic. Rather, like DuBois, he held strongly to the ideal that "all spheres of human endeavor should be free to his race." Nevertheless the composer greatly admired the revered educator. The feeling was evidently mutual. Washington contributed an illuminating preface to Taylor's Twenty-

Four Negro Melodies Transcribed for the Piano (op. 59), published in 1905 by the Oliver Ditson Company of Boston. The transcriptions were written as an invitation from the publishers in connection with his first visit to America in which he attempted to show the main currents of native Negro music.

The music is an interesting collection of diverse ethnic sources.* Four are from South-East Africa, two from South Africa, one each from West Africa and the West Indies, and the remainder from America. They are quite different in concept from the "rag-time" with which Coleridge-Taylor was familiar and had heard on his first American tour. He expressed in no measured terms his contempt for this style.

(In addition to the preface by Washington, which follows, the Twenty-Four Negro Melodies also contain a foreword by Coleridge-Taylor himself. †)

"Samuel Coleridge-Taylor"
by Booker T. Washington

'It is given to but few men in so short a time to create for themselves a position of such prominence on two continents as has fallen to the lot of Samuel Coleridge-Taylor. Born in London, August 15, 1875, Mr. Coleridge-Taylor is not yet thirty. His father, an African and native of Sierra Leone, was educated at King's College, London, and his medical practice was divided between London and Sierra Leone.

"As a child of four and five Coleridge-Taylor

---

*See Chapter Four, which is devoted to a discussion of Twenty-Four Negro Melodies.
†This, the most extensive article by the composer setting forth his comprehension of African and American Negro melodies, is reprinted on page 146.

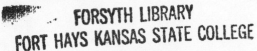

could read music before he could read a book. His
first musical instruction was on the violin. The piano
he would not touch, and did not for some years. As
one of the singing-boys in St. George's Church, Croydon, he received an early training in choral work. At
fifteen he entered the Royal College of Music as a student of the violin. Afterwards winning a scholarship
in composition he entered, in 1893, the classes of Sir
Charles Villiers Stanford, with whom he studied four
years or more.

"Mr. Coleridge-Taylor early gave evidence of creative powers of a high order, and to-day, at the age
of twenty-nine, he ranks as one of the most interesting and remarkable British composers and conductors.
Aside from his creative work, he is actively engaged
as a teacher in Trinity College, London, and as conductor of the Handel Society, London, and the Rochester Choral Society. At the Gloucester Festival of 1898
Mr. Coleridge-Taylor attracted general notice by the
performance of his Ballade in A minor, for orchestra,
Op. 33, which he had been invited to conduct. His
remarkably sympathetic setting in cantata form of portions of Longfellow's Hiawatha, Op. 30, has done much
to make him known in England and America. This
triple choral work, with its haunting melodic phrases,
bold harmonic scheme, and vivid orchestration, was
produced one part or scene at a time. The work was
not planned as a whole, for the composer's original intention was to set Hiawatha's Wedding Feast only. This
section was first performed at a concert of the Royal
College of Music under the conductorship of Stanford,
November 11, 1898. In response to an invitation from

the committee of the North Staffordshire Music Festival The Death of Minnehaha, Op. 30, No. 2, was written, and given under the composer's direction at Hanley, October 26, 1899. The overture to The Song of
Hiawatha, for full orchestra, Op. 30, No. 3, a dis-
tinct work, was composed for and performed at the
Norwich Musical Festival of 1899. The entire work,
with the added third part, --Hiawatha's Departure, Op.
30, No. 4, --was first given by the Royal Choral Society in Royal Albert Hall, London, March 22, 1900,
the composer conducting.

"The first performance of the entire work in America was given under the direction of Mr. Charles E.
Knauss by the Orpheus Oratorio Society in Easton, Pa.,
May 5, 1903. The Cecilia Society, of Boston, under
Mr. B. J. Lang, gave the first performance of Hiawatha's Wedding Feast on March 14, 1900; of Hiawatha's Departure on December 5, 1900; and on December 2, 1902, The Death of Minnehaha, together with
Hiawatha's Departure.

'In 1902 Mr. Coleridge-Taylor was invited to conduct at the Sheffield Musical Festival his orchestral
and choral rhapsody Meg Blane, Op. 48. The fact
that this work was given on the same program with a
Bach cantata, Dvořak's Stabat Mater and Tchaikovsky's
Symphonie Pathétique indicated the high esteem in
which the composer is held.

"A sacred cantata of the dimensions and style of
a modern oratorio, The Atonement, Op. 53, was first
given at the Hereford Festival, September 9, 1903,
under the composer's baton, and its success was even
greater at the first London performance in the Royal

Albert Hall on Ash Wednesday, 1904, the composer
conducting. The first performance of The Atonement
in this country was by the Church Choral Society under
Richard Henry Warren at St. Thomas's Church, New
York, February 24 and 25, 1904. Worthy of special
mention are the Quintet for Clarinet and Strings, Op.
6 (1897), which Joachim has given, and the Sorrow
Songs, Op. 57 (1904),--a setting of six of Christina
Rossetti's exquisite poems.

"Beside the works already mentioned are a Nonet
for Piano, Strings and Wind, Op. 3 (1894), Symphony
in A minor, Op. 7 (1895), Solemn Prelude for Orchestra, Op. 40 (1899), between thirty and forty songs,
various piano solos, anthems and part songs, and
works in both large and small form for the violin with
orchestra or piano.

"Mr. Coleridge-Taylor has written much, has
achieved much. His work, moreover, possesses not
only charm and power but distinction, the individual
note. The genuineness, depth and intensity of his feeling, coupled with his mastery of technique, spontaneity,
and ability to think in his own way, explain the force
of the appeal his compositions make. Another element
in the persuasiveness of his music lies in its naturalness, the directness of its appeal, the use of simple
and expressive melodic themes, a happy freedom from
the artificial. These traits, employed in the freedom
of modern musical speech, coupled with emotional power and supported by ample technical resource, beget
an utterance quick to evoke response.

"The paternity of Mr. Coleridge-Taylor and his
love for what is elemental and racial found rich

expression in the choral work by which he is best
known, and more obviously in his African Romances,
Op. 17, a set of seven songs; the African Suite for the
piano, Op. 35; and Five Choral Ballads, for baritone
solo, quartet, chorus and orchestra, Op. 54, being a
setting of five of Longfellow's Poems on Slavery. The
transcription of Negro melodies contained in this volume is, however, the most complete expression of Mr.
Coleridge-Taylor's native bent and power. Using
some of the native songs of Africa and the West Indies
with songs that came into being in America during the
slavery regime, he has in handling these melodies
preserved their distinctive traits and individuality, at
the same time giving them an art form fully imbued
with their essential spirit.

'It is especially gratifying that at this time, when
interest in the plantation songs seems to be dying out
with the generation that gave them birth, when the Negro song is in too many minds associated with 'rag'
music and the more reprehensible 'coon' song, that the
most cultivated musician of his race, a man of the
highest aesthetic ideals, should seek to give permanence to the folk-songs of his people by giving them a
new interpretation and an added dignity.

* * *

'Negro music is essentially spontaneous. In Africa it sprang into life at the war dance, at funerals,
and at marriage festivals. Upon this African founda-
tion the plantation songs of the South were built. According to the testimony of African students at Tuskegee there are in the native African melodies strains
that reveal the close relationships between the Negro

music of America and Africa, but the imagery and
sentiments to which the plantation songs give expression are the outcome of the conditions in America
under which the transported children of Africa lived.
Wherever companies of Negroes were working together,
in the cotton fields and tobacco factories, on the levees
and steamboats, on sugar plantations, and chiefly in
the fervor of religious gatherings, these melodies
sprang into life.

"Oftentimes in slavery, as to-day in certain parts
of the South, some man or woman with an exceptional
voice was paid to lead the singing, the idea being to
increase the amount of labor by such singing.

"The Negro folk-song has for the Negro race the
same value that the folk-song of any other people has
for that people. It reminds the race of the 'rock
whence it was hewn,' it fosters race pride, and in the
days of slavery it furnished an outlet for the anguish
of smitten hearts. The plantation song in America, although an outgrowth of oppression and bondage, contains surprisingly few references to slavery. No race
has ever sung so sweetly or with such perfect charity,
while looking forward to the 'year of Jubilee.' The
songs abound in Scriptural allusions, and in many instances are unique interpretations of standard hymns.

"The songs that had their origin in Virginia and
the more northern of the Southern States, where the
slave changed masters less often, and where he was
under the personal care and guidance of his owner,
are more bright and joyous in tone than are those
which were sung in the Gulf States, where the yoke of
slavery was more oppressive. The songs of the South

are sadder in tone, less buoyant than are those of the upper South.

"The plantation songs known as the 'Spirituals' are the spontaneous outbursts of intense religious fervor, and had their origin chiefly in the camp meetings, the revivals and in other religious exercises. They breathe a child-like faith in a personal Father, and glow with the hope that the children of bondage will ultimately pass out of the wilderness of slavery into the land of freedom. In singing of a deliverance which they believed would surely come, with bodies swaying, with the enthusiasm born of a common experience and of a common hope, they lost sight for the moment of the auction-block, of the separation of mother and child, sister and brother. There is in the plantation songs a pathos and a beauty that appeals to a wide range of tastes, and their harmony makes abiding impression upon persons of the highest culture. The music of these songs goes to the heart because it comes from the heart.

"The question is often asked to what extent are these songs being sung by the colored people and to what extent are they being preserved. In the larger city churches they are being used but little; but in the smaller towns, and in the country districts, where colored people live in greater numbers, their use is quite general, and new ones appear from time to time. Several schools and colleges of the South make an effort to preserve these songs, and at Fisk, Hampton and Tuskegee, they are sung constantly. New students coming from remote parts of the South occasionally bring in new ones. While some of the colored people

do not encourage the singing of the songs because they
bring up memories of the trying conditions which gave
them rise, the race as a whole realizes that apart
from the music of the Red Man the Negro folk-song is
the only distinctively American music, and is taking
pride in using and preserving it.

'It is, I repeat, a cause for special gratitude that
the foremost musician of his race, a man in the zenith
of his powers, should seek to chronicle, and thus perpetuate, the old melodies that are so rapidly passing
away.

"Mr. Coleridge-Taylor is himself an inspiration to
the Negro, since he himself, the child of an African
father, is an embodiment of what are the possibilities
of the Negro under favorable environment. In his preface to the Cabin and Plantation Songs, as sung by
Hampton students, Mr. Thomas P. Fenner said four
decades ago, 'The freedmen have an unfortunate incli-
nation to despise this music [Negro music] as a ves-
tige of slavery; those who learned it in the old time,
when it was the natural outpouring of their sorrows
and longings, are dying off, and if efforts are not
made for its preservation, the country will soon have
lost this wonderful music of bondage. It may be that
this people which has developed such a wonderful musical sense in its degradation will, in its maturity, produce a composer who would bring the music of the
future out of this music of the past. ' May we not look
to Samuel Coleridge-Taylor for a fulfilment of this
prophecy ?"

Booker T. Washington
Tuskegee Institute, Alabama
October 24, 1904

Chapter Four

TWENTY-FOUR NEGRO MELODIES*

Coleridge-Taylor felt that classical forms from sonata to symphony would be largely artificial and too civilized to superimpose upon Negro melodies. His main concern in transcribing melodies to pianoforte solos was first to present the theme of the song as a motto so that it would be readily recognizable. Then he would elaborate upon the motto through a series of variations and transformations. This technique was particularly successful with Coleridge-Taylor.

It is worth remarking that the composer sought authoritative sources for his melodies. During a time when ethnomusicology was at best only slightly researched, he sought what was, at the time, the best material. He found valuable material in the Jubilee Songs as sung by the Jubilee Singers of Fisk University, collected in the 1870s by Theodore F. Seward. These were published as an appendix to the Rev. G. D. Pike's Story of the Jubilee Singers. The text and music give important insight into the musical performance practices of the times. It was published in 1872.

Coleridge-Taylor was first introduced to the Jubilee Singers--later to be called the Fisk Jubilee Singers--in the

*Samples of the melodies of each of the 24 are given at the end of the chapter.

99

1890s during their London concert tours. He speaks of their
director, Frederick J. Loudin, with affection, as one "through
whom I just learned to appreciate the beautiful folk music of
my race, and who did much to make it known the world
over."

The second source of music came from Les Chants
et les contes des Ba-Ronga by Henri Junod. This interesting 19th-century collection provided the composer with au-
thentic material from the Ba-Ronga district which is on the
borders of Delgoa Bay, South Africa.

Coleridge-Taylor used six songs from the Junod collection. At the Dawn of Day ("Loko ku ti ga") is from
southeast Africa, and opens the 24 Negro Melodies. The
six-measure motto simply harmonized is followed by 30 measures of development and a return to the motto (13 measures).

The Stones Are Very Hard ("Maribye ma nonoha ngop-
fu") is also from southeastern Africa (and the Juno collection).
The African title is figurative and may mean "life is difficult." It is a simple ABA setting. The melodic line (C major) uses C-D-E-F-G and A, but no B, the leading tone.
The composer's harmonization often uses a B-flat. The 16-
measure A section, with a four-measure coda, utilizes the
full melody. The 20-measure B section is a variation and
is in the key of G Major. Although the melody is literally
repeated in C Major for the return of the A section, the
harmonization is different.

The third selection, Take Nabadji ("Thata Nabandji":
from Junod) is also from southeastern Africa. A vigorous
composition, it manifests rhythmic energy that sounds primitive. It demands a good feeling for accents, dynamics and
tempo variation.

A poignant southeastern-African lament, They Will Not Lend Me a Child ("A ba boleki nwana!"; from Junod) is marked andante lamentoso. It is a difficult rhapsodic work that varies its time signature and uses duple against triple figuration simultaneously. The composer explains, "The meaning of They Will Not Lend Me a Child is obvious. In countries where a childless married woman is considered less than nothing, it is only natural that such a one should try to borrow a child for adoption--a plan not, I believe, by any means unknown among more civilized peoples. Her lament on finding she is unable to discover a child is therefore literal in every sense of the word."

Coleridge-Taylor provides a footnote to his arrangement of Song of Conquest ("Ringendje"; from Junod) from South Africa. It is "a kind of song and dance not specially characteristic of the Ba-Ronga and possibly exotic." This is one of the most extended compositions in the 24 Negro Melodies and embraces 170 measures. Despite the title, the composer indicates the tempo as allegro molto and, in parentheses, molto leggiero (very lightly). The type of conquest is not clear but the ornate figurations and subtle interpretive changes give the music an exotic character.

Finally, the sixth melody from Junod is a Warriors' Song from South Africa. This 135-measure piece is also rhythmically complex. Its tempo is given as moderato alla marcia (moderate as in a march). The martial character is not immediately apparent, as Coleridge-Taylor does not always give a strong downbeat accent. There are two footnotes that deserve mention. In the first, the composer quotes the source as "heard on 'Negro Piano' in country of the Ba-Ronga played by natives." The second says, "The subject above is certainly not unworthy of any composer--

from Beethoven downwards. It is at once simple, strong
and noble, and probably stands higher than any other example
of purely 'savage' music in these respects."

Oloba, the seventh and final melody from Africa, was
given to the composer by Mrs. Victoria Randall, a family
friend. The melody is essentially pentatonic and is from
West Africa. The composer also placed a four-measure
rhythmic motif immediately after the Oloba melody, which is
a West African drum-call and was taken from his own personal collection. This is incorporated with the Randall supplied melody.

Clearly the most popular melody is the Bamboula, an
African dance that was transported to the West Indies. Bamboula is derived from bula, an African drum used to accompany a dance. In addition to Coleridge-Taylor, the American
composer Louis Moreau Gottschalk (1829-1869) also idealized
the Bamboula (op. 2). (It enjoyed a craze in Paris where
Gottschalk was a favorite pianist.)

This melody was also the groundwork for an orchestral rhapsody Coleridge-Taylor composed for Mr. and Mrs.
Carl Stoeckel (see Chapter Five) and the Litchfield, Conn.,
Music Festival. The composer described the rhapsody to
Stoeckel as "very brilliant in character, as you well see by
the subject, which is taken from my collection of 24 negro
melodies." It is a neglected miniature masterpiece and
could easily equal Scott Joplin's "Maple Leaf Rag" in popularity. (Coleridge-Taylor was in many ways the antithesis
of Scott Joplin. The Englishman expressed his contempt of
rag and "coon" music, considering the "rag-time" he heard
in his 1904 American tour a mongrel product in which the
most vulgar elements of White and Negro music are combined.) The melody was taken from a collection of the

noted music critic and historian Henry Edward Krehbiel
(1854-1923), who was for many years critic of the New York
Tribune. Krehbiel made the acquaintance of Coleridge-
Taylor during his American tours. In 1914, Krehbiel pub-
lished his collection of 527 songs as Afro-American Folk
Songs; A Study in Racial and National Music (New York, G.
Schirmer).

The Angels Changed My Name is the first of 16 melodies taken from the United States. These are quite different in mood from the African models, for they experienced
some transformation in a new land and reflected different
conditions. This melody was taken from Seward's Jubilee
collection. It begins with the eight-measure motto present-
ing the theme in somber rolled chords. A series of intricate variations follow. The diminished seventh chord, long
symbolic of emotional feeling, is effectively used in the concluding coda. It is a sad piece but very expressive.

There is an interesting letter dated May 16, 1905,
from Sir Charles Stanford to Coleridge-Taylor. After sug-
gesting that he send a copy to Percy Grainger who was very
interested in folk music, Stanford tells him "one of the tunes
The Angels Changed My Name is an Irish tune, and I also
think the Pilgrim Song. Like most of the negro tunes
Dvořák got hold of, these have reached the American negroes
through the Irish-Americans. A curious transmigration of
folk songs."

Coleridge-Taylor is particularly successful with his
adaptation of Deep River, a favorite melody of Harry Burleigh. Although the composer borrowed the melody from the
Jubilee book it was likely that he knew this popular melody
from hearing the Jubilee Singers during their London concerts. Deep River was also written as a violin solo, Slow

Movement on a Negro Melody, Deep River, as a tribute to
the Stoeckels. Rolled chords present the six-measured
motto. It is followed by good pianistic writing in a variety
of guises. The composer is quick to return to the motto in
a simple harmonic structure about one-third, and then about
two-thirds of the way. One feels that the tempestuous emotion must relax to clearly restate the expressive theme.

Didn't My Lord Deliver Daniel is also from Seward's
Jubilee Songs. It is followed by Don't Be Weary Traveler
which the composer simply referred to as "American Negro." Both were very well known melodies and it is very
likely Coleridge-Taylor knew and heard them from several
sources.

The Oliver Ditson Co., publisher of 24 Negro Melodies, was also the publisher of a popular collection, Jubilee
and Plantation Songs, from which the composer borrowed Going
Up, a joyous tune embellished with many grace notes and
rhythmic bounce.

I'm Troubled in Mind was a well-known plantation
hymn, which Coleridge-Taylor took from the Seward collection. Sayers relates in his book that the original tune was
taken from the lips of a slave in Nashville, who had just
heard it from her father. He does not relate the source of
information but goes on to say that after the old slave had
been whipped, he would sit down beside his cabin and sing
with such feeling that few could listen without sympathy.
This was a particular favorite of Coleridge-Taylor and he
used it as his theme and set of 14 variations in his Symphonic Variations on an African Air, op. 63.

The next transcription, I Was Way Down A-Yonder
("Dum-a-lum") gives no specific source, but the composer
gives the simple footnote, "one of the most characteristic

of American negro melodies. " It is a highly rhapsodic piece
and modulates quite freely. There is also a free-flowing
mixture of duple and triple meter; this is the only melody of
the 24 to show that characteristic.

Let Us Cheer The Weary Traveler, a simple but effective setting in C Major with a bright E Major modulation
in the middle was, again, taken from Jubilee Songs.

Coleridge-Taylor had many problems finding the proper melody for the slow movement, adagio, of his Violin Concerto, op. 80. After working with great difficulty with Keep
Me From Sinking Down, Good Lord, he changed to Many
Thousand Gone. It was to become the final theme of the
slow movement. The melody was taken from Ditson's Jubilee and Plantation Songs and is one of the most interesting
harmonizations in the 24 Negro Melodies.

My Lord Delivered Daniel was also taken from the
Ditson collection. It is bright allegro molto with many oc-
tave jumps and doublings.

Cabin and Plantation Songs was the source for Oh, He
Raise a Poor Lazarus, a slow expansive melody in C Minor.
This is a simple arrangement with the emphasis placed on a
melodic line simply stated without chords. The variations
are constructed very lightly, with an emphasis on the melodic contour.

The Pilgrim's Song and The Angels Changed My Name
were thought by Stanford to be of Irish genesis. Coleridge-
Taylor gives no source, but simply describes them as American Negro melodies. The text is quite well known: 'I'm
a poor way-farin' stranger, while journeyin' thro' this land
of woe. Yet there's no sickness, toil and danger, in that
bright world to which I go. " It is commonly considered a
White spiritual. Stanford was probably correct in his

assumption that this was the transmigration of a white (Irish)
melody into Negro culture.

Run, Mary, Run was the fourth and final melody taken
from Jubilee and Plantation Songs. The agitated melodic line
and text are reflected in rapidly moving figurations in the
piano, particularly broken chords (arpeggios). The left hand
has awkward jumps, perhaps to capture the nervous rush of
the story.

The shortest of the melodic transcriptions is Sometimes I Feel Like a Motherless Child. It is one of the sad-
dest of the spirituals. There is always the danger of over-
arrangement of spirituals and the adding of superfluous harmonic structures, but Coleridge-Taylor succinctly captures
the mood of this one through the use of rolled chords and
simple harmony. This brief but very well controlled arrangement is one of the easiest to play in the set.

Steal Away, although a simple melody, is expanded
by the composer to show a variety of transformations. This
arrangement in particular goes through a variety of key
changes: F Major, C Major, F Major, B-flat Major, A-flat
Major, F Major, C Major, and finally, F Major.

The 24 Negro Melodies concludes with an arrangement
of Wade in the Water taken from New Jubilee Songs. It is
one of the most difficult of the compositions, with rapid
passage work and rhythmic drive.

Fortunately the 24 Negro Melodies are still available
from the publisher. They are worth rediscovering. Coleridge-Taylor and his American Negro colleagues, Booker T.
Washington, W. E. B. DuBois, and Harry Burleigh, were
all concerned with the future of the Negro spiritual. In the
prefatory appreciation Washington said, "It is especially
gratifying that at this time, when interest in the plantation

songs seems to be dying out with the generation that gave them birth ... that the most cultivated musician of his race ... should seek to give permanence to the folk-songs of his people by giving them a new interpretation and an added dignity."

1. At the Dawn of Day

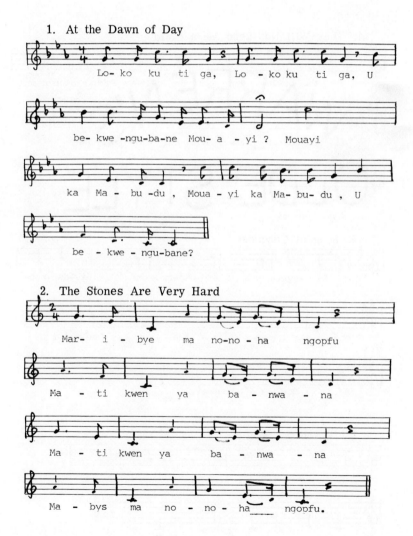

Lo- ko ku ti ga, Lo - ko ku ti ga, U
be- kwe -ngu-ba-ne Mou- a - yi ? Mouayi
ka Ma - bu -du , Moua - yi ka Ma- bu- du , U
be - kwe - ngu-bane?

2. The Stones Are Very Hard

Mar- i - bye ma no-no - ha ngopfu
Ma - ti kwen ya ba - nwa - na
Ma - ti kwen ya ba - nwa - na
Ma - bys ma no - no - ha ngopfu.

3. Take Nabandji

Tha - ta, na-ba - ndji, na-ba- ndji! Tha-

ta, na - ba -ndji, ba-na-ndji !

4. They Will Not Lend Me a Child

A ba bo-le-ki-nwa-na ! Ba bo-le-ka Fchu-rini nku-mba

Ngi ndi ma-nga Hu! Ngi ndi chi- mu ngwe,

Ngi- nba ku u - Ha!

5. Song of Conquest

Ri -nge - ndjé Dzé-dzé-rou-mbé. Dzé-dzé-rou-

mbé La pou-e - la a oua - ni Dzé-dzé-rou-

mbé, Dzé - dzé -rou-mbé.

6. Warriors' Song

7. Oloba

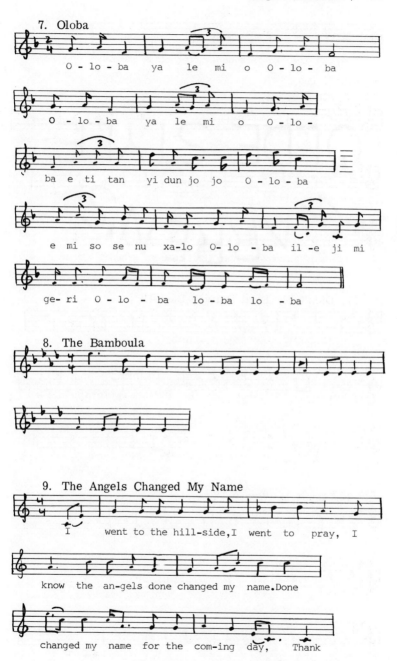

O - lo - ba   ya   le   mi   o   O - lo - ba

O - lo - ba   ya   le   mi   o   O - lo -

ba   e   ti   tan   yi   dun   jo   jo   O - lo - ba

e   mi   so   se   nu   xa-lo   O- lo - ba   il -e   ji   mi

ge- ri   O - lo - ba   lo - ba   lo - ba

8. The Bamboula

9. The Angels Changed My Name

I   went to the hill-side, I   went   to   pray,   I

know   the   an-gels   done   changed   my   name. Done

changed   my   name   for   the   com-ing   day,   Thank

God the an-gels done changed my name.

10. Deep River

Deep_____ ri - ver, my home is ov - er Jor - dan,____ Deep_____ riv-er, Lord I want to cross o-ver in - to camp ground.

11. Didn't My Lord Deliver Daniel?

Did-n't my Lord de-liv-er Dan - iel; D'liv-er Dan-iel__ d'liv-er Dan-iel, Did-n't my Lord de-liv-er Dan - iel,__ And why not a ev- 'ry man ?

12. Don't Be Weary, Traveler

Don't be wear - y trav- el - er, Come a - long home to Je - sus, Don't be wear-y trav - el - er, Come a-long home to Je - sus.

13. Going Up

Oh, yes , I'm going up , going up,

going all the way Lord, going up,

going up, to see the heav- en - ly Zland.

14. I'm Troubled in Mind

I'm trou-bled, I'm trou-bled,I'm trou-bled in

mind. If Je-sus don't help me, I

sure - ly____ will die.

15. I Was Way Down A-Yonder

I was way down a - yon - der a -

by my - self, I was hunt-ing a -

fo'some a - bo som a friend. A-way down

Dum a la dum-a-lum a dum-a-lum yon-der

Dum a la dum-a-lum a dum-a-lum   a - by my

Dum a la dum-a-lum a dum-a-lum self O

Dum a la dum -a-lum a dum-a-lum.

16. Let Us Cheer the Weary Traveler

Let us cheer the wear-y   trav-el-er

cheer the wear-y, trav-el-er   let us cheer the wear-y

trav-el-er   a - long the heav-en-ly   way.

17. Many Thousands Gone

No more auc-tion block for me, No more,

no more,   no more auc-tion block for me.

Man-y thous-and gone.

18. My Lord Delivered Daniel

My Lord de-lib-er'd Dan-iel, My

Lord de-lib-er'd Dan-iel, My Lord de-lib-er'd

Dan-iel: Why can't he de-lib-er me? I

met a pil-grim on de way; an' I ask him whar he's a

goin' I'm bound for Canaan's hap-py lan' an'

dis is deshouting band. Go on

19. Oh, He Raise a Poor Lazarus

Oh, He raise a poor La- za - rus,

Raise him up, He raise him from the dead, I

tol' ye so, while man-y were stand - ing

by_____ Je-sus loo-sen'_____ de

man from un-der_____ the groun' an' tell him: Go

pro-phe - - sy._____

20. Pilgrim's Song

I'm a   poor   way-far-in' stran-ger While journeyin'

thro' this land of woe. Yet there's no sick-ness,toil and

dan-ger In that bright world to which I   go.

21. Run, Mary, Run

Run, Mar-y, run , Run, Mar - y , run, Oh,

run, Mar - y, run, I know de   od-er worl'm

not like dis.

22. Sometimes I Feel Like a Motherless Child

Some-times I feel like a moth-er-less child,

Some-times I feel like a moth-er-less child. A

long ways from home. True be-liev-er. etc.

23. Steal Away

Steal a - way. Steal a -way . Steal a - way to

Je - sus ! Steal a -way , Steal a-way home. I

haint got long to stay here.

24. Wade in the Water

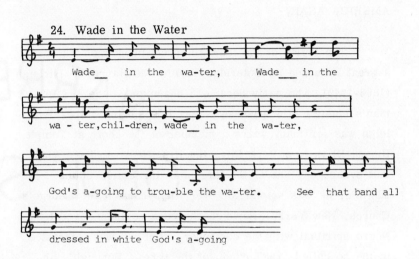

Wade__ in the wa-ter, Wade__ in the

wa - ter,chil-dren, wade__ in the wa-ter,

God's a-going to trou-ble the wa-ter. See that band all

dressed in white God's a-going

Chapter Five

AMERICA AGAIN

The fourth of the four American black men who had
a great influence on Coleridge-Taylor was Harry T. Burleigh
(1866-1949), who early became a champion of the Englishman's music. The possessor of a fine singing voice, Burleigh was for many years a member of the choir at Temple
Emanu-El in New York City, the first Negro to have sung in
that synagogue, one of the largest in the United States. In
addition, he was soloist for over fifty years at St. George's
Church, New York. Burleigh shared a common love of the
Negro spiritual with the composer. Neither was interested
in the so called "rag" music of the time. Burleigh's arrangements of spirituals were considered in the vanguard of
good taste. In addition, he also composed over 250 songs.

Coleridge-Taylor wrote a letter to Mr. Hilyer of the
Coleridge-Taylor Society in Washington on May 2, 1903, in
which he remarks with favor about Mr. Burleigh.

I have heard a great deal about Mr. Burleigh from
people I have met here who have heard him in the
States. Everyone agrees that he is a splendid singer and also--more rare--a splendid musician. Unfortunately the two things do not always go together.

Composer and singer met in Washington, D.C., during Coleridge-Taylor's first visit to America in 1904. They
shared a mutual admiration for Antonin Dvořák. Burleigh

116

had studied with the Czech master when he was director of the National Conservatory in New York.   There has been speculation that it was Burleigh who supplied Dvořák with the melodies of Negro origin that were introduced into the New World Symphony.

Coleridge-Taylor and Burleigh became close friends and were to appear together in subsequent concerts, particularly during the second tour of 1906.   The Anglo-black composer felt that the American black singer had an outstanding voice and dramatic instinct.   He felt that his talent was approached by only one other singer, Julien Henry.   Englishman and American were both committed to the full development of spirituals as the best expression of Negro music.

Coleridge-Taylor's American tour of 1906 included direction of several of his choral works and concerts in Washington, Pittsburgh, St. Louis, Chicago, Milwaukee, Detroit, Toronto and Boston.   The composer directed the Coleridge-Taylor Choral Society in The Atonement, The Quadroon Girl, and Hiawatha at the Metropolitan A. M. E. Church in Washington.   A brief tour with Burleigh was also arranged, beginning in New York's Mendelssohn Hall.   It was a recital of his smaller compositions and was repeated with little variation throughout the tour.   The program:

Violin Soli . . . . Mr. Felix Fowler Weir
   (a) "Intermezzo. "
   (b) "Entr'acte No. I. "
   (From the Music to Nero.)

Songs for Soprano . . . . Miss Lola Johnson
   (a) "The Young Indian Maid. "
   (b) "Beauty and Song. "

Songs for Baritone ... Mr. Henry [sic] T. Burleigh
   (a) "Love's Passing. "
   (b) "A Corn Song. "

Piano Soli .... S. Coleridge-Taylor
"Two Oriental Waltzes":
(a) Andante con Sentimento.
(b) Allegro Moderato.

Violin .... Mr. Felix Fowler Weir
"Romance in E Flat."

Songs for Soprano .... Miss Lola Johnson
(a) "Spring had Come."
(b) "Minguillo."

Songs for Baritone ... Mr. Henry [sic] T. Burleigh
(a) "She Rested by the Broken Brook."
(b) "Beat, Beat, Drums!"

Violin Soli .... Mr. Felix Fowler Weir
"African Dances":
1. Allegro Moderato.
2. Andantino (based on a real negro melody).
3. Allegro Vivace.
4. Allegro Energico.

This second tour was also the beginning of a warm
friendship with Mr. and Mrs. Carl Stoeckel and an association with the Litchfield County Choral Union at Norfolk, Connecticut. In recognition of Coleridge-Taylor's election as an
honorary member of this organization in 1906, during his
second American tour, he received an invitation before the
tour was ended to give a recital at the Village Hall in Norfolk, Connecticut. The program was a great success and
included a rising salute from the audience. The pleased
musician remarked, 'I will do anything but make a speech."
It was a strenuous tour but nevertheless most enjoyable, and
confirmed Coleridge-Taylor's belief that musical taste in the
United States was very good, which he attributed to the enormous German element in the large cities.

A review by Richard Aldrich of one evening's performance during this tour appeared in the New York Times

on November 17, 1906. It is perceptive but not overly enthusiastic. However, it would appear from the program that
the composer, who was not a virtuoso pianist, performed
his less brilliant and less significant compositions. These
were not necessarily his weaker works, but they did limit
the scope of the concert. Nevertheless, Aldrich offers an
interesting commentary (reprinted here from Aldrich's Concert Life in New York, 1902-1923, New York: G. P. Putnam's Sons, 1941):

'Nov. 17. Another distinguished foreign composer
appeared before a New York audience last evening,
swelling the list of those who have come to America
this season to exploit their own music. Mr. S.
Coleridge-Taylor came quietly, almost unheralded, but
his is a name which in England has been raised to
eminence by his work, though he is a young man and,
what will seem more remarkable in this country, a
mulatto. His concert last evening was devoted entirely to his own compositions, and he himself appeared
as a pianist. He has the modesty and the dignity of
the truly distinguished; and both he and his music
made a deep impression upon those who were there.

"The most important music he has composed, and
that upon which his fame chiefly rests, works in the
larger forms for chorus and orchestra, could not be
represented at this concert. Songs and pieces for the
piano and for the piano and violin made up the program, in which he had the assistance of Miss Lola
Johnson, soprano, Harry T. Burleigh, baritone, and
Felix Fowler Weir, violinist, all of his own race. Of
these Mr. Burleigh, who is well known as a singer in
this city, was the only one of artistic capacities really

sufficient for the demands made upon them.   Mr.
Coleridge-Taylor himself plays the piano with the skill
of a composer, not of a virtuoso, but he gave an admirable account of his piano pieces and played the accompaniments of his other works with taste and skill.
'His songs show a fine gift of melody and distinction in the harmonic treatment of the accompaniment.
Most characteristic and most valuable from a musical
point of view is his setting of Paul Laurence Dunbar's
'Corn song,' a reminder of antebellum days on a plantation in the South, with a Negro refrain.   In this he
has created an atmosphere and heightened the emotional
effect of the verses.   Mr. Burleigh sang it with sympathy and feeling and with uncommonly good enunciation.
Mr. Coleridge-Taylor played two of his 'symphonic
arrangements' of Negro songs for the piano (... I'm
Troubled in Mind and the West Indian Bamboula, of
which Gottschalk years ago made a once popular transcription).   There were also his Zuleika and an Oriental waltz.   The first two represent a most interesting
attempt to use the Negro folk-song material in artistic
music and have many successful and striking features.
The other songs and the violin pieces have not quite so
much that would call special attention to them, but they
are all admirable music and the work of sound and
original musicianship. "

The Third Visit

        In October of 1909, Carl Stoeckel was in England and
called upon the composer.   The philanthropist offered an invitation not only to conduct the first two parts of Hiawatha,
but to compose a new work for the Litchfield Festival during

a new American tour of 1910. Coleridge-Taylor accepted
and set about composing The Bamboula.

To celebrate the twentieth year of the founding of the
Choral Union, the members had reflected their preference
of a musical composition by ballot and Mr. Stoeckel had
promised to invite the composer to conduct it. The two top
selections were the Verdi Requiem and Hiawatha. Stoeckel's
happy answer was, "Well, circumstances effectually prevent
the appearance of Verdi, but we can get Coleridge-Taylor."

The third and final visit to America took place in
June of 1910. Stoeckel has written an interesting account
of the Litchfield Festival, and one of the fullest descriptions
of Coleridge-Taylor's personality available, in a letter to
W. C. Berwick Sayers (which appears in the latter's biography, Samuel Coleridge-Taylor, Musician; His Life and Letters,
1st ed. London: Cassell, 1915; 2d ed. London: Augener,
1927, p236-41).

"He reached this country in June, by way of Boston, came to New York, and I met him at the first rehearsal of the Bamboula Rhapsodic Dance, and the new
composition which he had made and brought with him,
and of which he had corrected the parts on board ship.
He leaned over from the conductor's stand as I came
up the aisle and shook hands, mopped his brow, and
remarked: 'This is a wonderful orchestra. I never
directed anything like it. They can read anything
beautifully at first sight.' And after the rehearsal the
men in the orchestra were quite as complimentary to
him. They called him the African 'Mahler,' as it is
generally conceded by orchestral musicians that the
greatest conductor who ever visited this country was
the late Gustav Mahler of Vienna, who was for some

time conductor of the Philharmonic Society of New
York. Before engaging the orchestra, I took the pre-
caution to sound the Musical Union as to whether there
would be any objection to playing under an Anglo-
African conductor. I was told that there would be no
objection, that he would come under the rule of 'visiting conductor.' He had three rehearsals in New York,
and then came with me to Norfolk. We had lunch on
the train from a hamper which we had taken precau-
tion to carry with us. We had plenty of wine in the
basket, but Mr. Coleridge-Taylor would not take any
of this, and, in fact, did not take a drop of wine or
liquor of any sort during the week that I was with him.
He drank ginger-ale, and smoked a moderate number
of cigarettes. Some months before his visit we had
informed the members of our society that he was coming, and that he was an Anglo-African, and if anybody
had any objection to singing under him would they please
state it at once. Of nearly eight hundred members
only one withdrew. One of the soloists, being of
Southern birth, also withdrew, but there were many
volunteers more than willing to take his place and to
have the prestige of performing the part under so
great a composer as Mr. Coleridge-Taylor. I suppose
that it is difficult for you in England and Europe generally to understand the unfortunate and unreasonable
prejudice which still exists against Africans in the
United States; but the fact is here, we must face it
and do our best to overcome it, and I know of no incident, in my life at least, that has done so much to
dissipate this feeling as the visit of Mr. Coleridge-
Taylor to this country in 1910.

"We had at Norfolk two rehearsals of the Hiawatha music. Four hundred and fifty singers were on the stage and four hundred and twenty-five in the audience. Mr. Paine, our conductor, made a speech of introduction, and then Coleridge-Taylor advanced to the conductor's platform. All the chorus on and off the stage rose, with vigorous clapping and shaking of handkerchiefs, and welcomed him. He was greatly pleased with his reception, but quickly settled down to business, and started off the rehearsals. As he said: 'It was a letter-proof chorus.' He had very few suggestions to make at either of the rehearsals with the New York Orchestra, of seventy-five pieces, and also the soloists. He had tried the soloists at our house in the afternoon, and was greatly pleased with the way in which Madame Alma Gluck sang her part. When he came from the library, where he had been rehearsing with her, he remarked to me in a low tone, 'That girl is the best Minnehaha I ever heard sing the part.'

"At the first concert we gave Verdi's Requiem Mass. Mr. Coleridge-Taylor was present, and was so good as to say to Mr. Paine that his rendition of the work had given him many new spiritual ideas that he had not observed before in the work. He was the only Anglo-African in the audience, and naturally attracted a great deal of attention, bearing himself with great dignity, modesty, and affability. The next night we gave the Indian music, and as the composer entered he was given the rising salute by two thousand people, who made great applause, which he acknowledged gracefully, and then we had a truly magnificent performance of his work. Everybody was in an enthusiastic and receptive state of mind, nobody more so than the composer himself, and when he came off the stage he said: 'I do not believe that my work has ever been better done, and I know that I have never directed it so well before, because I felt that everybody, the chorus, orchestra, and audience, were with me. This is one of the happiest days of my life.' There was a great demonstration again after the close of his work.

"My wife had invited a number of people to be our guests during the concert season and to meet Coleridge-Taylor, who also was our guest during his stay in Norfolk. We had a delightful supper party after the concert, at which the house party and other guests, to the number of twenty-five, sat down at the supper in honour of the composer. Some of the most prominent musicians of America, accompanied by their wives, were present at this supper, and several highly complimentary speeches were made to Coleridge-Taylor, eulogising him as a man and a musician. Knowing of his disinclination to make a speech, I did not ask him to say anything, but as we were about to leave the table he arose somewhat timidly and said: 'I never make speeches, but I do not feel as if I could leave this table without expressing the gratitude I feel for all which has been done for me by my hosts, the Litchfield County Choral Union and its conductor, Mr. Paine, and the others who have been so good as to be interested in my work. I never in my life have known anything like it. It has been simply royal, and I thank you.' We then adjourned to the library, where we had a jolly time and some impromptu music. The various composers, George W. Chadwick, Horatio Parker, and

Coleridge-Taylor, playing a lot of lively stuff, and Madame Gluck singing a number of African songs, in which our visitor was greatly interested.

"The next day we took an automobile ride, and got off of some of the main roads and drove through some of the fields of laurel (Kalmia), then in full blossom. Coleridge-Taylor was greatly delighted with the wild, picturesque scenery of northwestern Connecticut. When he came home that evening he retired at once to his room. When I went to call him for supper, I knocked on his door. He answered: 'Come in.' As I entered I saw him shoving some little sheets of musical notes into the desk. He said nothing about it at the time, but some months afterwards wrote me that these were his first sketches of A Tale of Old Japan, and that he had been inspired to make them by the floral display that he had seen that afternoon."

Mr. Stoeckel's letter to Sayers went on to say:

'In reference to the first performance of Hiawatha, under the conductorship of Sir Charles Villiers Stanford, Coleridge-Taylor told me that he listened to it from the outside, occasionally peeping into the room, but he felt too timid and fearful about its success to go into the hall. He also remarked several times: 'If I had retained my rights in the Hiawatha music I should have been a rich man. I only received a small sum for it.'

"While at our house he had breakfast in his room every morning, then came downstairs, and played on the piano for an hour, and then walked by himself or with me for an hour or two, strolling about or making calls. He was very particular about his personal appearance, being carefully groomed, and invariably putting on his gloves as soon as we issued from the house. He carried a small cane, and was apt to be smoking a cigarette. He became very fond of the tea which we have at our house, and also of the pens which my wife had placed on his desk, which he said were better than any he had used in England. At table he was rather a small eater, and quite careful of his choice of dishes. He always showed a lively interest in everything and everybody about him while at Norfolk. He did not ask many questions, as his pleasing personality and modest demeanor almost always resulted in drawing out those who conversed with him.

'In a conversation concerning contemporary music, Coleridge-Taylor spoke highly of Dvořák and Grieg. He did not seem to care much for most of the modern Russian music, saying that he had spent several pounds on scores, and wished he had the money back again. He did not include Tschaikowsky in this category, and spoke especially of Rimsky-Korsakoff, whose works he considered largely made up of brilliant and clever orchestration. He was much interested in some new works by American composers, notably those of Chadwick and Parker, which had been written for our festivals, and which were just fresh from the printers when he was here. He spoke of giving King Gorm the Grim, by Parker, and Chadwick's cantata, Noel, with some of his societies in England. I mention this as it shows his liberal and progressive disposition.

"One of his personal attributes was his graceful attitude when on the conductor's stand. This has been

commented on by great numbers of people who saw him
conduct here.   To see him on the conductor's stand
where he presented all the appearances of a well-re-
strained warhorse panting for the fray, was a contrast
from the appearance he made when he stood up to be
introduced at his first recital, and seemed almost to
shrink within himself--his diffidence made a marked
impression on the audience, who considered it pathetic;
but as soon as he was where there was anything to do
with music, he was all himself.

"He brought with him to this country what he termed
a conductor's jacket, and was particular about changing
from street attire into this jacket, although many of the
orchestra and most of our conductors, at that season of
the year at least, worked at rehearsals without coats.
I told him that it would be entirely good form if he
chose to work without his coat at rehearsals, but he
always went at once to his dressing-room and donned
his conductor's coat. "

*   *   *   *   *

The Final Years

Perhaps the finest work by Coleridge-Taylor is the
Violin Concerto, written as a consequence of his 1910 Amer-
ican tour and intended to be performed at the next Litchfield
County Choral Union Festival and for the Stoeckels.   The
concerto was completed just before the composer's death in
1912 and was first performed posthumously by Miss Maud
Powell, for whom it was expressly written, at Litchfield,
Connecticut, on June 4, 1912.   A very informative article,

one of the few scholarly treatments of the composer ever, was written for the Musical Quarterly (New York) in 1922 by Herbert Antcliffe, at a time when Coleridge-Taylor's music was very popular in the United States. In particular, Antcliffe gives informative background to the Violin Concerto and The Bamboula, in relationship to American Negro influences. A portion of that article follows:

"Being himself a violinist of no inconsiderable ability, it is not surprising that much of his most effective music, a Concert-stück, a Sonata, Four African Dances, two Ballades and many smaller pieces, were written with the violin as the principal instrument. Of these the most important, or at least the most ambitious, is the Violin Concerto in G minor, Op. 80. This was written during his first [i. e. , third] successful visit to the United States, and was based principally upon negro melodies, of which he had made a large collection. As it was commissioned by Carl Stoeckel and intended to be played by Maud Powell, Coleridge-Taylor not unnaturally endeavored to meet the ideas of these two, both of whom he recognized as musicians of a high order. One of their suggestions which he accepted was that he should use 'Yankee Doodle' as one of the principal themes, which he did by making it the second theme of the finale. Unfortunately neither this tune nor the original first theme of that movement inspired him to any real outburst of music, and the result was a movement that was scrappy and unsatisfactory, though not without some moments of beauty and some fine strong writing for both soloist and orchestra. Less pleased even than were his critics, the composer decided to lay the work aside, and had not better counsels prevailed it would probably have shared the fate of other unsatisfactory works and been consigned to the fire. On his return to England he decided to rewrite the work entirely, and in doing so discarded both themes and treatment of the last movement and used only short fragments from the second one. What the cause of dissatisfaction with this second movement was, it is difficult to see, for it is a piece of real beauty, based on the negro melody, 'Many thousand gone.' It is now published as a separate work. Possibly it was the same general feeling of dissatisfaction with what was done and of the great potentiality of what was to come which made him from time to time offer huge holocausts of manuscripts on the altar of efficiency and good work.

'In the new version of the first movement, in which he retained the principal theme as well as many of the details of the original work, and the finale stand out for their nobility, as well as for the effectiveness from the technical point of view of their rhythm and orchestration. We find in the themes, just as in those of some of his earlier works, melodic cadences which theoretically are feminine, but which in effect are not only virile but masculine. Very striking in this respect is the opening theme, which forms a strong contrast to its companion theme, the latter being actually and clearly feminine in its close, or the curiously piquant second theme of the finale. Although written some years later, there is a certain affinity between two of these and the principal melody of the orchestral Ballade, while it will be remembered that the same feminine cadence occurs again and again in the thematic material of The Song of Hiawatha.

"Another work commissioned by Stoeckel was an orchestral piece, for which he [Coleridge-Taylor] supplied the Bamboula, an early work rewritten with the experience of later years, and particularly with his increased knowledge of negro music. It gets its name as well as its principal motive from the dance melody well known from its association with the Negroes of the West Indies. What have probably done more to cause its popularity than anything else are the energy of its movement and the piquancy of its orchestration, for it carries the hearer along in a swirl of sound that never fails of sensation. Its cleverness is not so obvious as is that of some of his other works. Here he laid himself out to write a work which should be simple and popular, and achieved these characteristics in a marked degree. Not that it is in any way unworthy of its composer or lacking in real musicianship; but it is not a work which strikes the hearer as anything more than an able and interesting little number which most qualified musicians with a bent to constructive work could have written. Unlike many popular numbers by composers of higher powers, it helps towards popularity without detracting at all from his serious reputation. It preserves the original movement of the native dance, but also contrasts, and by doing so somewhat accentuates, its character with a theme that is more in keeping with conventional musical ideas, although even the contrasting theme is based on that with which it is contrasted. In this matter it bears a close resemblance to the Ballade."

* * * * *

Stoeckel's letter to W. C. Berwick Sayers (quoted earlier in this chapter) also contained an account of the creation of the Violin Concerto:

"After supper my wife went into the library, and Coleridge-Taylor and I went into another room to have a smoke. She began playing on the piano, and suddenly Coleridge-Taylor dropped his cigarette, jumped to his feet, and said: 'What is that lovely melody?' It was an African slave song called 'Keep Me From Sinking Down, Good Lord,' which has never been in the books, as it was taken from the lips of a slave directly after the war by a teacher who went south and who gave it to my late father-in-law, Robbins Battell. Coleridge-Taylor went into the library and asked my wife to play it again, which she did, singing the melody at the same time. He said: 'Do let me take it down. I will use it sometime.' For several days some of the violin passages in the Bamboula rhapsody had been running in my head, and the thought came to me that perhaps Coleridge-Taylor might be induced to write a violin concerto, using this African melody in the adagio movements. I proposed the matter to him then and there. He said that he was delighted with the idea, and would undertake it. He was, of course, to take his own time and to receive an honorarium therefor. In due season the manuscript of the violin concerto reached me. I took it at once to Madame Maud Powell, as the work was dedicated to her, and she was to give the first rendition. My original suggestion to Coleridge-Taylor was that the concerto should be

founded on three African melodies characteristic of our
so-called Southern negro airs. When we went over the
concerto, we found that the second movement was based
on an African melody, but not on 'Keep Me From Sinking Down,' which Coleridge-Taylor had found that he
could not use, and he had substituted 'Many Thousand
Gone' for this movement. In the third movement he
had used 'Yankee-Doodle' quite frequently, which, of
course, is not strictly an African melody. We agreed
that the second movement of the concerto was a beautiful piece of music, but both the first and the third
movements seemed to us rather sketchy and unsatisfactory. While I was considering what to write about
this work to Coleridge-Taylor, I received a letter from
him, requesting me to throw it into the fire; and saying that he had written an entirely new and original
work, all the melodies being his own, and that it was
a hundred times better than the first composition. I
returned his first composition to him at once, as it
seemed a pity to lose the second movement; and a few
weeks later the score of the second concerto arrived.
It was tried and found highly satisfactory. Its first
rendition was at the Norfolk Music Festival of 1912,
being played by Madame M. Powell, under the direc-
torship of Mr. Arthur Mees. After the first concerto
arrived, which we did not use, and which did not contain the air 'Keep Me From Sinking Down,' I wrote to
Coleridge-Taylor, and suggested that he should make
a separate arrangement of this air either for violin or
'cello. He responded with promptness, and sent along
with the second concerto an arrangement of the air for
violin and orchestra. This was played as an encore

by Madame M. Powell at the time of the rendition of
the concerto. "

*   *   *   *   *

The composer died, in Croydon, England, on September 1, 1912. The following is a tribute that Sir Hubert
Parry, principal of the Royal College of Music had published
in The Musical Times (London) October 1, 1912.

"The regret and even astonishment at the sudden
cutting short of a life brimming with artistic activity
will be so widely diffused that it would be a waste of
words to dwell upon it. There will be thousands who
will feel a sense of saddening loss when, in surround-
ings in which it had become familiar, they miss the
arresting face in which gentleness, humour, and modesty were so strangely combined with authoritative decision when matters of art were in question.

'It is to the general credit that people accepted
command and criticism from one whose appearance
was so strikingly unoccidental. The racial combination
could not leave people quite indifferent any more than
it could be indifferent in the artistic product. But
when Coleridge-Taylor came to the Royal College of
Music he was accepted on terms of full equality, and
soon won the affection of every one with whom he came
into contact. He began with composition and violin as
his principal subjects and was unusually proficient in
harmony, and ultimately became equally proficient in
counterpoint. Violin at length dropped out, and was
replaced by pianoforte and organ; but the pianoforte did
not progress very far, probably owing to the singular

structure of his hands; which looked as if it would have been impossible for him to attain much technique on a keyed instrument. But as a matter of fact he did play, and naturally played with artistic sense and feeling. His compositions before long poured out in a spontaneous flood, showing the influence of the composers who appealed to him most at different period. He passed through various phases, and for a short while was influenced by Brahms; but this influence more or less evaporated, and he came more under the influence of Dvořák, between whom and himself there was some racial analogy; but it is notable that what appealed to him was always of a high order; and he was inclined to attack the highest and most concentrated forms of art. Among over twenty compositions of his which were performed at College concerts were a String quartet in D minor, Fantasie-Stücke for string quartet, a Clarinet quintet, a Nonet for pianoforte, wind, and strings, and three movements of a Symphony in A minor. This stood him in good stead when he came before the world in his own special line, for he was permeated by the diction of the finest masters of his art, that an elevated style and distinction of artistic quality had become part of his outfit.

"The first performance of the first part of 'Hiawatha' in 1898, in the makeshift concert-room of the College, which was known as the 'tin tabernacle,' was one of the most remarkable events in modern English musical history. It had got abroad in some unaccountable and mysterious manner that something of unusual

---

Opposite page: the Coleridge-Taylor grave, Brandon Hill Cemetery, Croydon.

interest was going to happen, and when the time came
for the concert the 'tin tabernacle' was besieged by
eager crowds, a large proportion of whom were shut
out--but accommodation was found for Sir Arthur Sullivan and other musicians of eminence. Expectation was
not disappointed, and 'Hiawatha' started on a career
which, when confirmed by the production of 'The Death
of Minnehaha' at the North Staffordshire Festival in
the following year, 1899, and of a final section by the
Royal Choral Society in 1900, established it as one of
the most universally beloved works of modern English
music.

"By the time it came into existence the narration
type of musical cantata was getting discredited. But
Coleridge-Taylor was peculiarly fitted by racial combination to produce an exception to the conventional tendency. The primitive nature delighted in stories. He
himself said that he was mainly attracted to Longfellow's poem by the funny names in it. At any rate it
was simple, unanalytic, straightforward pleasure in
the simple story which appealed to him. He did not
thirst for intellectual analysis, for recondite problems,
or for odd and self-conscious effects. He wanted to
put down what welled up in him quite simply and
straightforwardly. Like his half-brothers of primitive
race he loved plenty of sound, plenty of colour, simple
and definite rhythms, and above all things plenty of
tune. Tune pours out in passage after passage, genial
and kindly and apt to the subject, and, in an emotional
way, often warmly and touchingly expressive. The
pure occidental composer would have gone wrong trying to do something subtle and uncanny to show the

fineness of his insight--and details would have got out
of gear. But Coleridge-Taylor had no such temptations.
The musical activity was so prompt in him that he had
no occasion for researchfulness. The balance of style
is perfectly maintained. It is in this that the inward-
ness of a very interesting situation may be recognised.
It was the very simplicity and unconsciousness of his
character which caused the racial motives and impulses
to be revealed so clearly. He had no occasion to conceal them; and the niche which he made for himself in
musical history derives its individuality from the frank-
ness with which he revealed the qualities which were
the inevitable outcome of an exceptional and interesting
combination of influences. "

Chapter Six

THE VIOLIN CONCERTO

The Concerto in G minor (for violin), op. 80, caused
Coleridge-Taylor many problems. He wanted to please both
his patron Carl Stoeckel and the American violinist, Maud
Powell, who was to give the first performance. He re-
spected their musical abilities and accepted their ideas for
melodies to be used in the concerto.

However, the composer found these melodic ideas,
including the spiritual, "Keep Me From Sinking Down," and
"Yankee Doodle" not to his satisfaction. On their part,
Powell and Stoeckel also ultimately found the concerto, in
particular the first and third movements, to be unsatisfactory.

The composer then substituted "Many Thousands
Gone" for "Keep Me From Sinking Down" in the second
movement. This proved to be satisfactory to all concerned.
He was also encouraged to make an arrangement of the replaced air for violin or cello. Coleridge-Taylor responded
with promptness and enthusiasm. The result was an arrangement for violin and full orchestra.

The rewritten concerto was almost entirely new in
its thematic material. The first movement, allegro maestoso,
uses two contrasting themes; both are highly reminiscent of
Negro melody but evidentally neither is an actual spiritual.

The first 14 measure theme in G Minor is stated by full orchestra and expanded slightly for an additional 18 measures.

First Theme, First Movement

This is followed by 30 measures with the violin of
the melodic statement of the theme. A <u>moderato</u> section
follows for soloist and orchestra that transforms the theme,
in a manner distinctive to the composer, into a variety of
harmonic and melodic ideas.

A bright, vivacious second theme follows. It is
marked <u>vivace</u>.

Second Theme, First Movement

The new theme bounces from soloist to orchestra. Again, the theme, like the first, is highly reminiscent of Negro melody but is not an actual quote. The composer continues to emphasize the strength of the first theme. However, he also uses the rhythmic pattern of the second theme which creates an interesting poly-rhythm.

This poly-rhythm is further manifested in a succeeding section, allegro moderato. At first the full orchestra restates the first theme for 24 measures, but for the concluding 82 measures the violin soloist develops the second theme with the orchestra again repeating snatches of the first.

The concluding section presents the opening 14 measure theme for full orchestra, followed by soloist, and leads into a cadenza for the soloist over a D pedal point. It is well-written violinistically, with characteristic runs, scale passages, and double and triple stops.

A concluding musical statement allegro moderato, momentarily in G major, returns to the principal theme.

First Theme for Violin

Herbert Antcliffe identifies these two themes as well as cadences as masculine and feminine. "We find in the themes, just as in those of some of his earlier works, melodic cadences which theoretically are feminine, but which in effect are not only virile but masculine. Very striking in this respect is the opening theme, the latter being actually and clearly feminine in its close, or the curiously piquant second theme of the finale. Although written some years later, there is a certain affinity between two of these and the principal melody of the orchestral Ballade, while it will be remembered that the same feminine cadence occurs again and again in the thematic material of the Song of Hiawatha. "

The second movement, <u>andante</u> <u>semplice</u>, is essentially a song without words. The beauty of the haunting melody, "Many Thousands Gone, " is used by Coleridge-Taylor. It is the only theme in the movement and is treated rhapsodically.

After a simple statement of the melody by full orchestra, the soloist enters with florid passage work which weaves around the melody, but only fleetingly capturing the theme. Next, the composer explores the melody in a variety of harmonic, melodic and key changes. He also reflects many subtle changes of tempo and mood. Finally, the soloist plays the spiritual melody in a simple manner.

Theme of Second Movement

This leads into a sprightly orchestral <u>andantino</u> which also manifests a change in meter from a lilting $\frac{6}{8}$ to a more martial $\frac{2}{4}$, and in a key change from B-flat major to G major.

After the statement of this theme (part of the Negro melody), the solo resumes with its own melodic treatment.

Theme in G Major

However, this is not for long, for Coleridge-Taylor then ornaments and develops the theme for soloist and orchestra. Particularly interesting are the fluctuating meter changes, duple and triple. Finally, for the concluding 26 measures, the orchestra has the theme while the violin solo weaves an intricate passage around it.

This is a very expressive movement and Coleridge-Taylor evidently found a quality inherent in the melody that was conducive to development.

After a short introduction, the third movement, an allegro molto in $\frac{3}{8}$ time begins immediately with a fast-moving ($\dot{\downarrow}$. =104) theme for the violin.

This sprightly, dance-like melody is treated in a manner highly characteristic of Coleridge-Taylor. The composer was fond of the metamorphoses of themes so familiar in many of his compositions, particularly <u>Hiawatha</u>. The orchestration is light, helping to support harmonic changes and rhythmic energy. After 76 measures of solo

First Theme, Third Movement

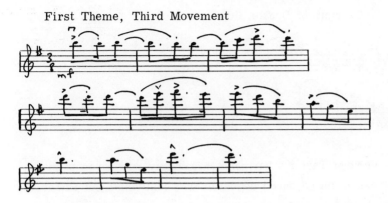

violin with orchestra, there is a brief 23-measure orchestral interlude which returns to the principal theme. The
following 45 measures with soloist is particularly free with
key changes and leads into a $\frac{2}{4}$ <u>moderato</u> section.

The second theme, lyrical in character, is stated by
the orchestra.

Second Theme, Third Movement

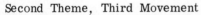

After the orchestral presentation, the violin enters.
The theme is fragmented with interlocking measures of
double stops.

The middle section of the third movement is a set
of intriguing variations based upon the first theme.   The
interest is maintained by unusual and abrupt key changes.

Example of Double Stops

Coleridge-Taylor's harmonic vocabulary was never to progress to an advanced degree of chromaticism, but rather,
he leaned toward picturesque and unusual key changes, colorful orchestration and fascinating transformation of melody.

The concluding section of the concerto returns to the
haunting first theme of the first movement.

First Movement Theme

This is developed orchestrally.   But it also transforms itself into the first theme of the third movement.
The violin reenters to play this theme again.   The musical
material following is almost a literal quote of the beginning

of the third movement but with some new key changes and harmonies. The lyrical second theme also is recapitulated, but is interrupted with brilliant cadenza-like passages. Finally a grandioso conclusion of the first theme is returned and leads up to the brilliant, effective conclusion.

Chapter Seven

COLERIDGE-TAYLOR'S WRITINGS

Coleridge-Taylor had a dislike for making speeches, writing articles or protesting with letters to the editor. Very few of these manifestations survive. However, there are just enough to shed light on the composer's philosophy of music and in particular his protestation of derogatory remarks regarding his Negro blood and heritage. The first item to follow is the Foreword, dated December 17, 1904, in London, to his Twenty-Four Negro Melodies (the music itself is discussed in Chapter Four).

THE FOREWORD

"The Negro Melodies in this volume are not merely arranged--on the contrary they have been amplified, harmonized and altered in other respects to suit the purpose of the book. I do not think any apology for the system adopted is necessary. However beautiful the actual melodies are in themselves, there can be no doubt that much of their value is lost on account of their extreme brevity and unsuitability for the ordinary amateur.

"What Brahms has done for the Hungarian folk-music, Dvořák for the Bohemian, and Grieg for the Norwegian, I have tried to do for these Negro Melodies. The plan adopted has been almost without exception that of the Tema con Variazioni. The actual melody has in every case been inserted at the head of each piece as a motto. The music

146

which follows is nothing more nor less than a series of variations built on the said motto. Therefore my share in the
matter can be clearly traced, and must not be confounded
with any idea of 'improving' the original material any more
than Brahms' Variations on the Haydn Theme 'improved' that.

"A word of explanation may not be out of place regarding the meaning of some of the Melodies--particularly
those from Africa, which have in some instances no words
to guide the reader. Some of the titles may be taken figu-
ratively; thus, 'The stones are very hard' may mean, 'Life
is difficult,' or that the path which the singer was treading
at the time was really stony. The meaning of 'They will
not lend me a child' is more obvious. In countries where a
childless married woman is considered less than nothing, it
is only natural that such an one should try to borrow a child
for adoption--a plan not, I believe, by any means unknown
among more civilized peoples. Her lament on finding she is
unable to discover a child is therefore literal in every sense
of the word.

"There is a great distinction between the African Negro and the American Negro Melodies. The African would
seem to be more martial and free in character, whereas the
American are more personal and tender, though notable ex-
ceptions to this rule can be found on either side. One of the
most striking points regarding this music is, in the author's
opinion, its likeness to that of the Caucasian race. The
native music of India, China and Japan, and in fact all non-
European music, is to our more cultivated ears most unsatisfactory, in its monotony and shapelessness. The music of
Africa (I am not thinking of American Negro music, which
may or may not have felt some white influence) is the great
and noteworthy exception. Primitive as it is, it nevertheless

has all the elements of the European folk-song and it is remarkable that no alterations have had to be made before
treating the Melodies. This is even so with the example
from West Africa--a highly original number. One conclusion may be safely drawn from this--the Negro is really and
truly a most musical personality. What culture may do for
the race in this respect has yet to be determined, but the
underlying musical nature cannot for a moment be questioned.

'I should like to acknowledge the valuable material I
have obtained from Monsieur Henri Junod's excellent and
sympathetic little book 'Les Chants et les Contes des Ba
Ronga.' Also I am indebted to Mrs. Victoria Randall for
the only specimen of West African music. Nor must I forget the late world-renowned and deeply lamented Frederick
F. Loudin, manager of the famous Jubilee Singers, through
whom I first learned to appreciate the beautiful folk-music of
my race, and who did so much to make it known the world
over. "

*   *   *   *   *

Coleridge-Taylor delivered an extempore address
from notes when he distributed the prizes to the students at
the Streatham School of Music in November, 1905. It was
one of the very few speeches he ever made. A fairly full
newspaper report appeared and it is from this that the text
is taken.

ON MUSIC

'I do not think that the study of what I may term the
unpractised side of music--by which I mean harmony, counterpoint, sight-reading, and extemporisation--can be too
strongly insisted on for all who are studying music, what-
ever branch it may be. It is remarkable that in these days

speciality, musicians, at any rate, are travelling in the
other direction, and are becoming broader instead of narrow-
er. While saying this, of course I do not forget that the
old style of music master, who teaches piano, violin, organ,
'cello, guitar, mandoline, banjo, singing, and a few other
subjects, is becoming a thing of the past--luckily for all of
us. I mean broader in another sense. The expert in one
practised subject is more often than not highly accomplished
in the side-lights of his art. I think it would be difficult to
name a single great, or even good, violinist or pianist of
the present day who is not also fully equipped with a technique for composition, though he may not be able to compose. They are all masters of harmony, counterpoint, ex-
temporisation and the orchestra, and the art is all the better
for it, though they may not be able to use these practically.
Organists I need not mention, because with them the study
of theory is a practical thing. An organist without a knowledge of harmony is not an organist. He cannot get on without it, whereas any other kind of instrumentalist may do so.
But there is one class of musicians to whom these subjects
are of especial use. I refer, of course, to singers. It is
astonishing that good musicianship so rarely goes hand in
hand with a good voice. For some reason or other, singers
seem to think that all their short-comings in this respect
will be forgiven so long as they have good voices. To
many, the poor person whom they call their 'coach' is
someone, good-tempered, who will literally draw the notes
of all their parts into their heads. This is all very well,
providing things go straightforwardly and without accident
when the singer is before the public. But when something
happens--and in our complex music something usually does
happen--where is the vocalist who is not better for a

thorough grasp of the whole work instead of his or her little part? I can illustrate the point from my own experience at a musical gathering in the North of England, when a soprano, who was not strong on the theoretical side, got slightly ahead of the orchestra in a composition in which, at a certain point, occurred a six bars' rest. For a time all went well, but when the lady attempted to proceed there were some rather unpleasant sounds. Singers, therefore, should acquire a good knowledge of theory to save themselves from any contretemps of this kind. Sight-reading, again, ought to be much more practised, though in this respect things are at a very high level in the North. I was adjudicating at the great Blackpool Festival, and for the sight-reading competition two choirs of about a hundred voices each entered. Copies of things they had never seen before were put into their hands--not easy things, by any means--and no one was allowed to look inside until the bell rang, on which they had to start away. First they sang without words, then with words and expression, etc. The winning choir sang the piece almost perfectly the second time. I think there are few choirs around London that could do anything of the sort --and all of these were amateurs. This brings me to another thought--there are people naturally gifted, many of them, who oppose a set study of harmony because it naturally results in dullness and commonplace respectability. Some little time ago I was reading a book of travel on the districts which border Europe and Asia. The writer--I have forgotten his name--mentioned that large bands of gipsies were to be found in the neighbourhood, and that in each band one could always discover at least three or four excellent violinists and guitar players, not to mention singers. The writer went on to say that these fiddlers and singers were wonderful in transposing melodies into words, and that this discovery gave him a shock, as it seemed to point to the fact that music was a very low and brainless accomplishment; otherwise, how could these people excel as they did? I posted the message to a friend, and casually remarked that they would not be worse musicians if they had a knowledge of the scientific side of the art. To which my friend replied that were they to study such things as harmony, etc., they would be better off. But I warn you not to allow harmony and theory to cramp your artistic development, because it should be remembered that these must always be subservient to the beauty of the sound. Therefore, those who are studying harmony should take care that these excellent things become not the end, instead of means to an end, and that they are not mere mechanical paper work, without any regard to sound. I have had a number of pupils who were able to work a difficult paper with ease, but who could not distinguish the most simple chords played in succession on the piano. Too often a wonderful knowledge of textbook harmony deprives the person who possesses it of the enjoyment of mere beauty, and this is a great pity. Imagination should also be far more thought of than it is in the playing of music. Technique is not everything, and everyone has some small amount of imagination. But imagination wants bringing to the front. We want to get away from the dull, conventional, respectable and matter-of-fact performances, and to go in for something better. We require less of the lady and gentleman, and more of the man and woman. We must look upon music from a more impersonal standpoint--there is too much of the everlasting heralding going on. It is becoming too much admiration for the man, and too little love for his music. I appeal for more enthusiasm. "

*   *   *   *   *

An article was written by the composer for The Etude
in January, 1911.   This American music journal was for
many years well known and popular and included not only reviews and news, but articles of scholarly interest.   Coleridge-
Taylor contributed this article as a result of his third visit
to America.

IS TECHNIQUE STRANGLING BEAUTY?
(From an English Point of View)

" 'You English musicians always seem to be thinking.
Why do you not sometimes feel also?'

"So remarked a Spaniard after having heard a particularly advanced specimen of the modern school of composition, and both statement and question seem to the writer to
be very pertinent.

"There appears to be a most desperate craving for
technical dexterity in music, and all other sides of the art
are being woefully left to take care of themselves.   Simplicity, the greatest proof of real strength, is for the time
being, at all events, in hiding, ashamed and afraid.

"Undoubtedly the most striking thing about the work
of the men of the younger school (and I refer throughout to
this new and younger school) is the wonderful ability, one
may say genius, in orchestration.

"For the young composer to have a complete mastery
of the most complicated machine in the world--the modern
orchestra--is the rule and not the exception, and the once
weakest spot in the equipment of the English composer is
now the strongest.

'It is now the fashion in the London musical smart
set to decry Tschaikowsky, but this extraordinary improve-
ment in English orchestral writing is distinctly traceable to
the influence of that great man--at any rate, it commenced

immediately after the advent of the Symphonie Pathétique, which work was, until quite recently, far more often heard than any of the composer's other compositions.

"Most English composers of fifteen or twenty years ago were content to use the organ-pedal-like bass in the orchestra, and the majority of the scores were drab and colourless things.

"This cannot be wondered at, perhaps, considering that so many writers held church appointments, for church music has had a tremendous influence on all music in England; and unlike other countries, there has never been any real operatic hold, until recently, to counteract it.

"But even then, it is strange that nothing much happened to orchestral technique till the time I have mentioned, for there were hundreds of beautiful French scores in existence, not to speak of those of Wagner himself. The explanation may lie in the fact that Wagner's scores were all music-drama and the French mostly operas and suites, so the type may have been considered foreign and operatic, and therefore not exactly suitable material from which the English composer could get hints for this particular kind of work. There may have been some truth in the supposition, but be that as it may, miserably rigid harmonies--even more rigid and monotonous bass parts, and orchestration without life or meaning were often the hall-marks of the English school of some years back.

"All this has been blown away as if by magic, and we have come to what? One of the most extraordinary positions imaginable!

'With the wonderful advance in general technique and orchestral writing, there seems to have come a deliberate

stamping out of everything melodically beautiful, and too often there is an utter absence of charm.

"Not only is much of the music of the young English
school devoid of what is commonly called 'tune,' but in nine
cases out of ten there seems to be no melodic outline.
Chaotic design, harsh, meaningless harmonies, an almost
overwhelming complexity, together with a brilliant score,
seem to form the watchword of much of the present-day
work. And it is this brilliant orchestration, combined with
an apparent want of melodic invention, warmth and real
charm, that is so astounding a feature. Complexity is not
necessarily a sign of great strength; on the contrary, it often denotes weakness.

"It is very easy to call the slow movement of the
New World Symphony of Dvořák (a composer, by the way,
shamefully neglected in London) 'a commonplace hymn tune';
but how many composers who are adepts at combining twelve
or more 'melodies' could write anything half so poetic, half
so beautiful and moving? How many of their melodies would
stand the test of being heard alone, out in the sunlight, as
it were, with only a few simple harmonies to support them?
For few recent compositions really move one--though many
of them astonish. It seems as if the composers would wish
to be classed with the flying man in his endeavours to 'go
one better' than the last, somehow or other, and in many
ways much of the music of the period reminds one of the
automobile and the airship. It is daring, clever, complex
and utterly mechanical.

"The question is--Should an imaginative Art follow
such lines? Should it not rather come from the heart as
well as the brain?

"Of course, a fine technical equipment is a very desirable thing, and nothing of worth can be accomplished without it; but should 'What do you think of my cleverness?' be stamped so aggressively over nearly every score that we hear?

"The lack of human passion in English music may be (personally I think is) merely transitory. It is being pushed aside only while the big technical Dread-nought is in its most engrossing stage of development. Soon the builders will have the time to love again--when the turmoil is hushed somewhat --to give the world a few tender and personal touches amidst the strife, which will 'make us feel again also. '

"And my Spanish friend will be happy once more!"

* * * * *

Coleridge-Taylor was always the articulate teacher. Accounts from his pupils and colleagues attest to his fine craftsmanship, good relationships and thoroughness. On November 12, 1907, the composer delivered a brief address to the prize students at the Beckenham and Bromley School of Music that is of interest regarding music education and the study of harmony, in particular.

THE ADDRESS

"There are many things connected with music that I might talk about, but as I recently examined the harmony papers of this school I shall confine my remarks to that most important subject, and the one or two things that arise directly from it. That every student--whatever his or her subject--should study harmony and counterpoint thoroughly goes without saying. There are some people, perhaps, specially gifted, who really appreciate the ins and outs of original and beautiful harmonies without knowing anything of

technique, but they are very much in the minority. It should
be remembered that the great difference between music and
the other arts (with the exception of dramatic poetry) is that
the former always requires a third person--that is to say, a
medium--between the composer and the listener. To argue
that the third need know nothing of the composition from a
harmonic or structural point of view is obviously ridiculous,
but whether audiences are better left in the dark or not is a
question I should not care to answer. But I will mention a
matter which often comes under my notice. I very frequently adjudicate in Wales and the North at eisteddfod meetings.
Six choirs, say, will sing one composition; now an audience
applauds for two things--a liking for the music itself, and
an appreciation of the rendering of the music. I will take
the position of the first and last choirs. The people, when
they hear the first choir, have not begun to like the composition very much--on the other hand, they have not had a
chance to compare renderings, so a certain amount of applause is granted. Things go on until the last choir sings.
By this time the audience know and like the music, and are
inclined to applaud much more on that score, but at the
same time are ten thousand times more critical as to the
renderings, because they have had a good chance of compar-
ing one rendering with another; consequently about the same
amount of applause is given, but, as you will see, for a
very different reason. That is why most adjudicators insist
that the audience's reception of the various choirs is the
very worst basis on which to give marks. A certain knowledge of harmony would cure to a great extent such mistakes
on the part of the listeners.

"Many students do harmony perfectly well on paper,
but if they are asked to name those very same progressions

when played on the piano, they are completely lost.   That,
it seems to me, is the main reason why harmony is considered a dull thing by so many students, a thing to be got
over quickly, and with as little trouble as possible--it means
nothing to them as regards sound.   In many cases it is all
but impossible for the professor to do anything in that way
at lessons, because harmony is generally taught in a class,
and there is consequently no time to spare.   I strongly ad-
vise harmony students to go through their work carefully on
the piano after they have done it as well as possible on the
paper, and to alter anything that sounds unmusical even
though it be correct, taking care, of course, that no new
mistakes are made by so doing.   On the other hand, a student should not rely on the piano, and ought to be able to
do a correct and fairly musical paper away from the instrument.   A fairly advanced student ought also to try to ana-
lyse the piece he or she is studying.   Harmony would not
then seem to be (as it so often does) a thing apart from the
voice or instrument, but something very much connected with
it indeed.

'Harmony, too, it [sic] is of great use to those who would
read at sight.   It is doubtful if anything is so really useful
to the musician as that.   To the orchestral player it is, of
course, imperative, and it is astonishing to find what a
splendid lot of good amateur violinists there are who can
read at sight.   But with pianists and vocalists it is another
matter.   How humiliating it must be to the pianists who,
after playing a Liszt rhapsody, on being asked to accompany
a simple song, has to 'own up. '   Seriously, many singers
tell me how impossible it is to sing some of the more modern songs of such writers as Strauss, Debussy, and Hugo
Wolf at concerts, because of the accompanists.   In these

overcrowded times it would surely be a good thing in every way if some of the young pianists made a special study of this. The tendency with modern composers is to make their piano parts quite as important as the solo. Accompaniments are no longer a placid background for the display of the soloists, and yet, notwithstanding this, it is very rarely that one meets the soloist who cares to go through the music more than once with the accompanist; therefore, the accompanist who would succeed today must, in addition to being a good pianist technically, have a complete grasp of the whole thing. Singers are by far the worst people in that respect. The inability of even good professionals to keep a part in a quartet, for instance, is one of the most disconcerting things a conductor has to get used to. Nearly all conductors are afraid of the singer coming in too early, or too late, or not at all; or, if a proper moment, then on the wrong note."

*   *   *   *   *

Coleridge-Taylor was an apostle of his color. This was reflected in many musical compositions. The man, several times too often, experienced unfortunate expressions of ill will because of his race. He often responded with music. But an incident in February, 1912, at Purley, England was particularly upsetting to him. At that time, a lawyer addressed a debating society about "The Negro Problem in North America." The session was presided over by a clergyman. The newspaper report which reached Coleridge-Taylor contained many derogatory ineptitudes and arrogance. The musician was upset and angry and protested to the Croydon Guardian.

LETTER TO
THE EDITOR OF THE CROYDON GUARDIAN

"Sir,

'I hear that the next subject for discussion at the

'Purley Circle' is to be 'God and His great mistake in cre-
ating Black Men,' with Jack Johnson in the chair.

"This meeting will be almost as interesting as the
last meeting, at which (as I gather from your report) a
clergyman-chairman actually thanked a lecturer for expressing not only un-Christian but unmanly sentiments about the
race in question. Doubtless the 'Purley Circle' is working
up for a lynching in the near future. I hope I shall be a
mere spectator and not the victim! Shame on the lecturer,
and a thousand times on the clergyman! And yet there was
a vast amount of humour in some of the things that were
said at that meeting. The smell of the negro, for instance.
All uncivilised people smell for a very obvious reason--they
do not wash. But what about the smell of the lecturer's
own ancestors who ran about half naked some centuries ago?
Was it that of a June rose? I wonder!

'It is amazing that grown-up, and presumably educated, people can listen to such primitive and ignorant non-
sense-mongers, who are men without vision, utterly incap-
able of penetrating beneath the surface of things.

"No one realises more than I that the coloured people
have not yet taken their place in the scheme of things, but
to say that they never will is arrogant rubbish, and an in-
sult to the God in Whom they profess to believe. Why, I
personally know hundreds of men and women of negro blood
who have already made their mark in the great world, and
this is only the beginning. I might suggest that the 'Purley
Circle' engage someone to lecture on one Alexandre Dumas,
a rather well-known author, I fancy, who had more than a
drop of negro blood in him. Who is there who has not read
and loved his Dumas? And what about Poushkin, the poet?

And Du Bois, whose 'Souls of Black Folk' was hailed by
James Payn as the greatest book that had come out of the
United States for fifty years? I mention these three because
not only are they distinguished men, but men of colossal
genius. And will the lecturer refer to a chapter in H. G.
Wells's 'Future of America,' called 'The Tragedy of
Colour'?--this, because Wells is undoubtedly possessed of
the heaven-born gift of insight to a greater degree than any
other living Englishman--not even excluding G. B. S.

"The fact is that there is an appalling amount of ignorance amongst English people regarding the negro and his
doings. If the Purley lecturer (I forget his name, and am
away from home, the Birmingham people having engaged me
to direct something that has come out of my ill-formed
skull)--I say, if he is right, then let us at once and for ever
stop the humbug of missions to darkest Africa, and let the
clergy stop calling their congregations 'dear brethren,' at
any rate whenever a black man happens to be in the church.
Let us change our prayer books, our Bibles, and everything
pertaining to Christianity, and be honest.

"Personally, I consider myself the equal of any white
man who ever lived, and no one could ever change me in
that respect; on the other hand, no man reverences worth
more than I, irrespective of colour and creed. May I further remind the lecturer that really great people always see
the best in others? It is the little man who looks for the
worst--and finds it. It is a peculiar thing that almost without exception all distinguished white men have been favour-
ably disposed towards their black brethren. No woman has
ever been more courteous to me than a certain member of
our own English Royal Family, and no man more so than
President Roosevelt.

'It was an arrogant 'little' white man who dared to say to the great Dumas: 'And I hear you actually have negro blood in you!' 'Yes,' said the witty writer; 'my father was a mulatto, his father a negro, and his father a monkey. My ancestry began where yours ends!'

"Somehow I always manage to remember that wonderful answer when I meet a certain type of white man (a type, thank goodness! as far removed from the best as the poles from each other), and the remembrance makes me feel quite happy--wickedly happy, in fact!

"Yours, etc.,

"S. Coleridge-Taylor.

"Midland Hotel, Birmingham"

Appendix A

CATALOG OF MUSIC BY COLERIDGE-TAYLOR

Samuel Coleridge-Taylor did not give an opus number
to all his compositions. This is particularly true with the
songs, anthems and other short choral works. Most of his
music is out of print. It is still possible to find a few
works available in recent editions, or to find the longer
choral, instrumental and orchestral works in antiquarian
book stores or music specialist stores.

It was often common for Coleridge-Taylor to make
arrangements of his music for scoring other than the original. For example, he made an arrangement of Ethiopia Saluting the Colours, op. 51, originally for orchestra, for
pianoforte solo. Often his friends J. Read and W. Henley
would, with the approval of the composer, prepare editions
with fingerings of violin arrangements. It was also a common English publisher's practice at the time to issue choral
music with tonic sol-fa signs.

This catalog of compositions by Coleridge-Taylor is
divided into four sections:

(1) A listing by opus number, that is, by order of
publication. The information includes the opus number,
name of the composition, year of writing and publication,
the instrumentation or voicing, the original publisher, date

163

and place of first performance. In addition, when possible, information is provided regarding unusual features of the music, source of texts, original press reviews or contemporary information and any other material that is of interest. Also, in many instances, the duration of the music is given.

(2) A listing of non-opus-number works--songs, choral works and other compositions--together with supporting information, whenever possible, regarding text, first performances, and unusual features.

(3) Arrangements by Coleridge-Taylor, or by friends with his approval, during his lifetime. This was a popular practice of the time. Many composers were pleased to make available their music in arrangements. After Coleridge-Taylor's death, his various publishers saw fit to issue editions of his music in various arrangements, including the popular English concept of "Salon Orchestras." The composer, his music, and arrangements, some indeed quite removed from the original concept, were particularly popular between World War I and World War II. The selected list includes many of these arrangements during this period.

(4) A list of compositions that are currently available in publishers' catalogs, for purchase or rental, including catalog or edition numbers, particularly since 1945.

1. THE LISTING BY OPUS NUMBER

Op. 1   QUINTET IN G MINOR (ms.). For pianoforte, two
          violins, viola and violoncello. Little is known about
          this work.

Op. 2   NONET IN F MINOR (ms.). Written in 1894, un-
          published. For pianoforte, violin, viola, violoncello,

double bass, clarinet, horn and bassoon. A student
work, it was first performed on July 5, 1895, at
the Royal College of Music. Sir George Grove was
in the audience with Col. Walters and both were
highly impressed. Sayers relates that Grove felt
the andante was too florid and too quick. He turned
to Walters saying, "He will never write a good slow
movement until he has been in love. No one can
who has not been in love. "

Op. 3 SUITE DE PIÈCES. Written in 1895 as a student
work, published in 1895 (?) by Schott. Pieces for
violin and organ or pianoforte. In four movements:
1. Pastorale, 2. Cavatina, 3. Barcarolle, 4. Con-
templation. Not much is known about the Suite.

Op. 4 BALLADE IN D MINOR. Written in 1895, published in 1895 by Novello. Written for violin and
orchestra. Dedicated "to my friend, Ruth Howell."
The first of three ballades; each for a different combination of instruments.

Op. 5 FANTASIESTÜCKE. Written in 1895; not published
until 1921 by Augener. String quartet: two violins,
viola and violoncello. In five movements: 1. Prelude in E Minor (Allegro ma non troppo), 2. Serenade in G Major (Andante molto), 3. Humoresque in
A Minor (Presto), 4. Minuet and Trio in G Major
(Allegro moderato), 5. Dance in G Major (Vivace).
First performed on March 13, 1895, at the Royal
College of Music. The Serenade and Dance are
perhaps the best movements, and were the most successful with the audience that first performance.

Op. 6 Unknown; title missing.

Op. 7 ZARA'S EAR-RINGS (ms.). Possibly composed in 1894, unpublished. A Rhapsody for soprano and orchestra. First performed February 7, 1895, at a college concert at the Imperial Institute, and sung by Miss Clementine M. Pierpoint. It is based on Lockhart's Spanish Ballads. Coleridge-Taylor liked, as he did later in Hiawatha, the queer sounding names. Op. 7 exhibited a fine craftsmanship of orchestration which would always be an outstanding feature of his music.

Op. 8 SYMPHONY IN A MINOR (ms.). Written in 1896, unpublished. The ms. is at the Royal College of Music. Written for full orchestra. First performed on March 6, 1896, at the Royal College of Music in St. James' Hall. The second movement is called Lament and is thematically partly based on a Negro melody, the first such inspiration. The last movement of this work gave the composer many problems. Stanford rejected four versions. It is provocative to see the different versions in the neat penmanship with the corrections by Stanford in great evidence. Ultimately a fifth version of the last movement was written and performed on April 30, 1900, at The Winter Gardens, Bournemouth.

Taylor's friend W. J. Read recovered the fourth rejected ms. from a fireplace immediately after the composer had dismissed it. Afterwards, Coleridge-Taylor used the theme from this rejected movement in his Melody for F for the organ.

Op. 9 TWO ROMANTIC PIECES. Written in 1896; published in 1896 by Augener. An edition of 1908 was edited and had fingering by J. Henley. For violin and pianoforte in two movements: 1. Lament and 2. Dance-Merrymaking. First performed on March 6, 1896, at the Royal College of Music.

Op. 10 QUINTET IN A MAJOR FOR CLARINET AND STRINGS. Written in 1895 and published by Breitkopf (Germany). It is presently available from Musica Rara, London. Written for clarinet, two violins, viola and violoncello in four movements: 1. Allegro energico, 2. Larghetto affetuoso, 3. Scherzo, Allegro leggiero, 4. Finale, Allegro agitato. First performed July 11, 1895, at the Royal College of Music. About 30:00.

Taylor first heard the Brahms Quintet for Clarinet and Strings op. 115, on March 13, 1895, and was immediately inspired by the combination of instruments and the music. Op. 10 is a well constructed work for what is generally considered a difficult combination. The slow movement contains an accidental quote from The Midsummer Night's Dream by Mendelssohn. Coleridge-Taylor's quintet was written as a college exercise for Sir Charles Stanford who brought it to the attention of the great Berlin violinist, Joachim, who found it thoroughly interesting and promising.

Dr. Stanford challenged Coleridge-Taylor and several other students to write the quintet and "keep it clear of Brahms." The completed work drew from Stanford the satisfactory "You've done it, me bhoy" [sic].

Op. 11 Unknown; title missing.

Op. 12 SOUTHERN LOVE SONGS. Written in 1896; pub-
lished in 1896 by Augener. Songs with pianoforte
accompaniment in five movements: 1. My Love (A
Spanish Ditty, lyrics by Longfellow), 2. Tears (A
Lament), 3. Minguillo ("Ancient Spanish," lyrics by
Lockhart), 4. If Thou Art Sleeping, Maiden (from
the Portuguese, lyrics by Longfellow), 5. Oh! My
Lonely Pillow ("Stanzas to a Hindu Air," lyrics by
Byron). Dedicated to Miss Mamie Fraser.

Op. 13 QUARTET IN D MINOR (ms.). Written in 1896, unpublished. For two violins, viola and violoncello.

Op. 14 LEGEND FROM THE CONCERTSTÜCK. Written in
1893; published by Augener in 1897 and also in 1908
with bowing and fingering by J. Henley. For violin
and orchestra. Dedicated to Miss Marie Motto.
Coleridge-Taylor and his wife to be, Jessie S.
Fleetwood Walmisley, met for the first time when
she accompanied the violinist at the piano during a
private family gathering when this composition was
performed.

Op. 15 LAND OF THE SUN. Written in 1897 (?); published
in 1897 (?) by Augener. Part song (SATB) with
pianoforte accompaniment. Dedicated to Sir Walter
Parrett. Text taken from Byron's "Bride of Aby-
dos." 8 pp.

Op. 16 HIAWATHAN SKETCHES. Written in 1896; published by Augener in 1908 with fingering by W. Henley. Written for violin and pianoforte in three
movements: 1. A Tale, 2. A Song, 3. A Dance.

First performed in the Salle Erard in 1896 in a
joint concert with Paul Laurence Dunbar. It was
his first venture into the Hiawatha legend. The review in the Musical Times (vol. 36, 1897, p465)
was very enthusiastic: "We cannot find space to do
more than generally express our astonishment at a
composer barely out of his teens who produces work
after work showing remarkable originality in almost
every bar."

Op. 17 AFRICAN ROMANCES. Written in 1897; published
in 1897 by Augener. Songs with pianoforte accompaniment in seven movements: 1. An African Love
Song, 2. A Prayer, 3. A Starry Night, 4. Dawn,
5. Ballad, 6. Over the Hills, 7. How Shall I Woo
Thee. Dedicated to Miss Helen Jaxon. The lyrics
are by Paul Laurence Dunbar; this was the first
major work that was a collaboration between poet
and composer.

Op. 18 MORNING AND EVENING SERVICE IN F MAJOR.
Written in 1890; published in 1899 by Novello. Sacred service for S. A. T. B. chorus and organ, originally published in Novello's Parish Choir Book.
In five liturgical sections: 1. Te Deum, 2. Benedictus, 3. Jubilate, 4. Magnificat, 5. Nunc Dimittis.
Te Deum was the first, written in 1890 when Taylor was 15. Pages of music: 14; 10; 7; 9; 5.

Op. 19, No. 1. MOORISH TONE-PICTURES. Written in
1897; published in 1897 by Augener. Solo for pianoforte. In two movements: 1. Andalla and 2. Zarifa.

Op. 19, No. 2. LITTLE SONGS FOR LITTLE FOLKS. Written in 1898; published in 1898 by Boosey. Written for voice and pianoforte. Six songs: 1. Sea Shells, 2. A Rest by the Way, 3. A Battle in the Snow, 4. A Parting Wish, 5. A Sweet Little Doll, 6. Baby Land. Dedicated to my little sisters and brothers, Alice, Marjorie and Victor. The texts are by Cooper and Charles Kingsley.

Op. 20 GIPSY SUITE. Written in 1898, published in 1904 by Augener. Written for violin and pianoforte in four movements: 1. Lament and Tambourine, 2. A Gipsy Song, 3. A Gipsy Dance, 4. Waltz.

Op. 21 PART-SONGS. Written in 1898; published in 1898 by Augener. Written for three-part chorus (SSC). Two songs: We Strew These Opiate Flowers (Text from Shelley's Hellas) and How They So Softly Rest (words by Longfellow, after Klopstock). First performed December 16, 1898, at The Public Hall, Croydon.

Op. 22 FOUR CHARACTERISTIC WALTZES. Written in 1898; published in 1899 by Novello. For orchestra: 3222/4231 timp. tri. b. dr. cym. /str. In four movements: 1. Valse Bohémienne (Allegro ma non troppo), 2. Valse Rustique (Tempo di valse), 3. Valse de la Reine (Andante con sentimento), 4. Valse Mauresque (Furioso). First performance, December 16, 1898, at The Public Hall, Croydon. Coleridge-Taylor sent Jessie four subjects in musical notation for the Characteristic Waltzes as a token of love. These are not ballroom dances but subjects treated in waltz rhythm as Brahms had done. 13:00. 49 pp. of full score.

Op. 23 VALSE CAPRICE. Written in 1898; published in 1898 (?) by Augener. Written for violin and pianoforte.

Op. 24 IN MEMORIAM. Written in 1898; published in 1898 by Augener. Set of songs, subtitled "Three Rhapsodies for Low Voice and Pianoforte." In three movements: 1. Earth Fades! Heaven Breaks on Me (lyrics by Robert Browning), 2. Substitution (lyrics by Elizabeth Barrett Browning), 3. Weep Not, Beloved Friends (lyrics by Chiabrara). Probably first sung by Paul Laurence Dunbar.

Op. 25 DREAM LOVERS. Written in 1898; published in 1898 by Boosey. An operatic romance for two male and two female characters, chorus and orchestra. First performance, December 18, 1898, in the Public Hall, Croydon. The libretto is by Dunbar. The story is about a Madagascan prince and a quadroon lady who first meet in a dream. They recognize one another in real life, immediately fall in love, and wed. The performers were friends of the composer; the chorus was organized by Coleridge-Taylor and his Conservatoire class served as the orchestra. The vocal score is 37 pp. Long Years Ago from Op. 25 was particularly popular during Taylor's lifetime. Piano-vocal score 37 pp.

Op. 26 THE GITANOS. Written in 1898; published in 1898 (?) by Augener. A cantata-operetta for female voices, soli and three-part chorus with pianoforte accompaniment. Text by Edward Oxenford. This is a bright and melodious school cantata. 'Isola" from The Gitanos as arranged by Ernest Reeves became a very popular solo.

Op. 27 Unknown; title missing.

Op. 28 SONATA IN D MINOR. Written in 1898-9; published in 1917 by Hawkes. For violin and pianoforte, edited by A. Sammons.

Op. 29 THREE SONGS. Written in 1899; published in 1899 by Augener. Songs with pianoforte accompaniment in three movements: 1. Lucy (lyrics by Wordsworth), 2. Mary (lyrics by Wordsworth), 3. Jessy (lyrics by Robert Burns).

Op. 30, No. 1. HIAWATHA'S WEDDING FEAST. Written in 1898; published in 1898 by Novello. Cantata for tenor solo, chorus and orchestra. First performed November 11, 1898, at the Royal College of Music. 32:00.

Op. 30, No. 2. THE DEATH OF MINNEHAHA. Written in 1899; published in 1899 by Novello. Cantata for soprano and baritone soli, chorus and orchestra. First performed October 26, 1899, at the North Staffordshire Musical Festival, Hanley. 40:00.

Op. 30, No. 3. OVERTURE TO THE SONG OF HIAWATHA. Written in 1899; published in 1899 by Novello. Written for full orchestra. First performed October 6, 1899, at the Norwich Musical Festival. 4:00. The overture has no pictorial intention, and does not describe Hiawatha in any way. Taylor used the Negro melody, "Nobody Knows the Trouble

I See" in the overture. The composer recognized that this was an independent work and that its relationship to the cantatas is nominal.

Op. 30, No. 4. HIAWATHA'S DEPARTURE. Written in 1899-1900; published in 1900 by Novello. Cantata for soprano, tenor, and baritone soli, chorus and orchestra. First performed February 22, 1900, by the Royal Choral Society, Royal Albert Hall. 40:00. Famous soprano solo: "Spring Had Come. "

Op. 31 THREE HUMORESQUES. Written in 1897; published in 1897 by Augener. For orchestra: 3222/4231/ timp. cym. /str. Also written for pianoforte solo. In three movements: 1. D Major, 2. G Minor, 3. A Major. Written during the courtship of Coleridge-Taylor and Jessie and also during a period of separation.

Op. 32 Unknown; title missing.

Op. 33 BALLADE IN A MINOR. Written in 1898; published in 1898 by Novello. Written for full orchestra: 3222/4231/timp. cym. /str. First performed September 14, 1898, at the Three Choirs Festival in Gloucester, conducted by Coleridge-Taylor. Dedicated to August J. Jaeger, musical advisor to the firm of Novello and Musical Times critic. The title was given by the composer's wife when she was checking orchestral parts for her husband. 15:00. 63 pp. of full score. The Ballade was a great opportunity for Coleridge-Taylor and he was completely prepared. It was also through the kindness and admiration of Sir Edward Elgar that the commission was given to him. A letter from Sir Edward to Dr.

Herbert Brewer, of the Committee of the Three
Choirs Festival in 1898 read as follows: "I have
received a request from the secretary to write a
short orchestral thing for the opening concert. I
am sorry I am too busy to do so. I wish, wish,
wish you would ask Coleridge-Taylor to do it. He
still wants recognition, and he is far and away the
cleverest fellow amongst the young men. Please
don't let your committee throw away the chances of
doing a good act. "

Op. 34 Unknown; title missing.

Op. 35 AFRICAN SUITE. Written in 1898; published in
1898 by Augener. In four movements: 1. Introduction, 2. A Negro Love-Song, 3. Valse, 4. Danse
Nègre; numbers 1-3 were originally for pianoforte
solo and 4 was originally (ms.) a quintet for pianoforte and strings, although Coleridge-Taylor himself
orchestrated "Danse Nègre" (which was published in
1901 by Augener). "Danse Nègre" was first performed at a concert of the Croydon Conservatoire,
possibly in 1898. The inspiration for it came from
the poem of the same title by his good poet-friend,
Dunbar. This vigorous and entertaining work is currently available on a Columbia Records--Black Music Series recording. 20:00 (Danse Nègre: 5:30).

In common with his idol Dvořák, Coleridge-Taylor
held that great racial music is to be found in germ
in the folk-songs of a people. The Suite is Negro
in intention, even though it is not literally quoting
ethnic melody.

Op. 35, No. 2. HOW THEY SO SOFTLY REST. Published
in 1898 by Augener. Three-part song for female
voices with pianoforte accompaniment. The words
are by Longfellow, after Klopstock.

Op. 36 Unknown; title missing.

Op. 37 SIX SONGS. Written in 1898; published in 1899 by
Novello. Written for voice and pianoforte. Six settings: 1. You'll Love Me Yet (Robert Browning),
2. Canoe Song (Isabelle Crawford), 3. A Blood-Red
Ring Hung Round the Moon (Barry Dane), 4. Sweet
Evenings Come and Go, Love (George Eliot), 5. As
the Moon's Soft Splendour (taken from "To a Lady
Singing to Her Accompaniment on the Guitar," by
Shelley), 6. Elëanore (Eric Mackay). First performed February 24, 1898, by Miss Walmisley at
the Croydon Conservatoire (first four). "Elëanore"
was to become one of his most popular songs, including many recordings.

Op. 38 THREE SILHOUETTES. Written in 1899; date of
publication by Ashdown unknown. Solos for pianoforte in three movements: 1. Valse, 2. Tambourine,
3. Lament.

Op. 39 ROMANCE IN G. Written in 1899; published in
1900 by Novello. For violin and orchestra. First
performed May 24, 1899, at Salle Erard, London,
by Coleridge-Taylor, accompanied by Jessie at the
pianoforte.

Op. 40 SOLEMN PRELUDE. Written in 1899; published in
1899 by Novello. For full orchestra. First performed September 13, 1899, for the Three Choirs

Festival at Worcester. Dedicated to Paul Kilburn
of Bishop Auckland, Conductor of the Sunderland
Choral Society. Novello's did not like Coleridge-
Taylor's original title, "A Solemn Rhapsody." It
was changed to "A Solemn Prelude" with the composer's leaving the meaning of the title intentionally
vague. The composer was also the conductor at the
first performance and received a fine public reception.

Op. 41, No. 1. SCENES FROM AN EVERYDAY ROMANCE.
Written in 1900; published in 1900 by Novello. Written for full orchestra. Suite in four movements:
1. E Minor (Allegro), 2. G Major (Andante), 3. B
Minor (Tempo di valse), 4. E Minor (Presto).
First performed on May 24, 1900, by the Philharmonic Society at Queen's Hall, London, 12:00; full
score 37 pp. Despite the title, there is no pro-
grammatic content to the music. Joseph Bennett
wrote the program notes and described it as a symphony in miniature.

Op. 41, No. 2. NOURMAHAL'S SONG AND DANCE. Written in 1900; published in 1900 by Augener. Solos
for pianoforte. In two movements: 1. Nourmahal's
Song and 2. Nourmahal's Dance.

Op. 42 THE SOUL'S EXPRESSION. Written in 1900; published in 1900 by Novello. Four sonnets for contralto solo and orchestra or pianoforte in four movements: 1. The Soul's Expression, 2. Tears, 3.
Grief, 4. Comfort. First performed September 13,
1900, at the Hereford Musical Festival. Dedicated

to Marie Brema. Text: "Four Sonnets," by Elizabeth Barrett Browning.

Op. 43 THE BLIND GIRL OF CASTEL-CUILLÉ. Written in
1900-1901; published in 1901 by Novello. There is a
revised edition by the composer published in 1902.
Cantata for soprano and baritone soli, chorus and
orchestra. First performed on October 9, 1901, at
the Leeds Musical Festival, conducted by Coleridge-
Taylor with Mme. Albani and Andrew Black as soloists. The poem was translated from "The Gascon
of Jasmin," by Henry W. Longfellow. Dedicated "to
my friend, Nicholas Kilburn, Esq."
This was considered the wrong text for Coleridge-
Taylor by many friends, including Sayers and Stanford. The critics praised the work but with reservations and there were the inevitable comparisons
with Hiawatha. The story concerns Margaret, a be-
trothed girl who loses her sight. Her lover is unfaithful and prepares for marriage with Angela.
Margaret in frustration and sadness goes to church
where the ceremony is to take place with a knife so
that she can stab herself before her lover. But before she is able to do this, she falls dead at his
feet. The story had none of the elements that Taylor loved and composed so well: primitive romance,
forests, rivers, lakes, skies and pagan human sentiment.

Op. 44 IDYLL. Written in 1901; published in 1901 by Novello. Written for full orchestra. First performed
September 11, 1901, at the Gloucester Musical Festival. 5:00.

Op. 45 SIX AMERICAN LYRICS. Written in 1901; published in 1903 by Novello. Written for contralto or baritone and pianoforte accompaniment in six movements: 1. O Thou, Mine Other, Stronger Part (lyrics by Ella Wheeler Wilcox), 2. O Praise Me Not (Wilcox), 3. Her Love (Wilcox), 4. The Dark Eye Has Left Us (lyrics by Whittier), 5. O Ship That Sailest (Wilcox), 6. Beat, Beat, Drums (lyrics by Walt Whitman). Coleridge-Taylor probably had Jessie's voice in mind when he wrote these.

Op. 46 TOUSSAINT L'OUVERTURE. Written in 1901; published in 1901 (?) by Novello. Concert overture for orchestra: 3222/4231/timp. perc. /str. First performed October 21, 1901, at the Queen's Hall Symphony Concerts, conducted by Henry Wood. The personality of Toussaint appealed to Coleridge-Taylor: a slave who became a soldier, saved Haiti from invasion, and as its president restored order and prosperity, only to be finally crushed by Napoleon. The overture does not have obvious Negro themes, but is a subjective appreciation and study of Toussaint's character. There are four themes: the first and third are stern and strong and the second and fourth are gentle. 15:00.

Op. 47, No. 1. INCIDENTAL MUSIC TO HEROD. Written in 1900; published in 1901 by Augener. Incidental music for orchestra: 3222/4230/timp. perc. /str. This was the first of five commissions Coleridge-Taylor would receive to write music for London productions of Beerbohm Tree. Four of these were to texts by Stephen Phillips: Herod, Ulysses, Nero

and Faust. The fifth and last production was
Shakespeare's Othello. These were sumptuous productions and in a style that Taylor greatly enjoyed.
The published version used four of the musical settings: Professional, Breeze Scene, Dance, Finale.
12:45. There was also a song "Sleep, Sleep, O
King" which was published from the score. The
Musical Times review (vol. 41, no. 694 [Dec. 1,
1900], p818) records the following: "The time is
past when incidental music at our theaters was a
reproach, our managers now employ our best composers to write the music. "

Op. 47, No. 2. HEMO DANCE. Written in 1900; published
in 1900 by Novello. Scherzo for full orchestra:
3222/4230/timp. perc. /str. 7:00.

Op. 48 MEG BLANE. Written in 1902; published in 1902
by Novello. "A Rhapsody of the Sea," for mezzo-
soprano solo, chorus and orchestra. First performed on October 3, 1902, at the Sheffield Musical
Festival, conducted by Henry Wood. Coleridge-
Taylor succeeded Wood as conductor of the festival.
The sombre and rhapsodic poem is by Robert Buchanan. This dramatic composition was written after a visit to Hastings on the Sea. Buchanan's
poem had been in his mind for some time, and
probably these lines from the poem were of imme-
diate inspiration: "Hither and thither, thick with
foam and drift, / Did the deep waters shift, /
Swinging with iron clash on stone and sand. " The
brief poem describes some fisher-folk who stare
through a severe storm at a shipwreck. The ship

has been grounded upon a reef. A woman, Meg
Blane, and several other brave souls try to rescue
the stranded people on ship. They are overwhelmed
by a great wave which completely destroys both their
rescue and the wreck. The opening prologue is a
mezzo-soprano solo. After a short orchestral interlude, the chorus sings the descriptive story. This
section also includes another solo. The epilogue is
a literal repetition of the prologue, but is written
for divided choral writing (SSAATTBB) and soloist.

Op. 49 INCIDENTAL MUSIC TO ULYSSES. Written in 1901;
published in 1902 by Novello. Written for full orchestra. The original publication included only three
vocal selections: two songs for tenor, "Great Is He
Who Fused the Might" (drinking song) and "O Set
the Sails, " and a chorus for women (part song for
SSA and pianoforte), "From the Green Heart of the
Waters" (nymph's song). The entire score was first
performed in January 1902 for a Beerbohm Tree
production with text by Stephen Phillips at Her Majesty's Theatre. The music consisted of an overture, interludes, entr'actes, the two songs, part
song and a remarkably dramatic and effective storm
scene. The conductor Adolf Schmid felt Coleridge-
Taylor was an ideal composer for the theater.

Op. 50 THREE SONG-POEMS. Written in 1902-3, published in 1905 by Enoch. Three songs with pianoforte accompaniment in three movements: 1. Dreaming for Ever, 2. The Young Indian Maid, 3. Beauty
and Song. Lyrics by Thomas Moore. 18 pp.

Op. 51 ETHIOPIA SALUTING THE COLOURS. Written in
1902; published in 1902 by Augener. Concert march
for full orchestra. First performed by the Croydon
Orchestral Society, Coleridge-Taylor conducting.
This composition was dedicated to the Treble Clef
Club, Washington, D. C. , and has a Walt Whitman
quote on the cover, "Who are you, dusky woman,
so ancient, hardly human, with your woolly-white
and turban'd head, and bony feet? Why rising by
the roadside here, do you the colour's greet. "

Op. 52 FOUR NOVELLETTEN. Written in 1902; published
in 1903 by Novello. Written for string orchestra,
tambourine and triangle. In four movements: 1. A
Major, 2. C Major, 3. A Minor, 4. D Major.
Taylor greatly admired the Serenade by Dvořák and
this might have served as inspiration for his own
Novelletten. 21:00.

Op. 53 THE ATONEMENT. Written in 1902-1903; published
in 1903 by Novello. Sacred cantata for soprano,
mezzo-soprano, contralto, baritone and tenor soli,
chorus and orchestra. First performed on September 9, 1903, at the Hereford Musical Festival. The
text was by Alice Parsons, a member of the Three
Choirs and wife of a Cheltenham journalist. It is
musically and textually divided into five sections:
Prelude, Gethsemane, Prayer of the Holy Women
and Apostles, Pontius Pilate, Calvary. Vocal score
190 pp. There was a revised edition by the composer also published by Novello, in 1904. The soloists at Hereford were Mme. Albani, Emily Squire,
Kirkby Lunn, Andrew Black and William Green.

Op. 54 FIVE CHORAL BALLADS. Written in 1904; published in 1904-5 by Breitkopf. For baritone solo, chorus and orchestra. In five movements for SATB: 1. Beside the Ungathered Rice He Lay, 2. She Dwells by Great Kenhawa's Side, 3. Lord He Sang the Psalm of David, 4. The Quadroon Girl (with baritone solo), 5. In Dark Fens of the Dismal Swamp. First performed on October 25, 1905, at the Norwich Musical Festival, but written for and first performed in the United States by the Samuel Coleridge-Taylor Choral Society in Washington. The lyrics are from Poems on Slavery by Longfellow. Coleridge-Taylor composed an alternate version of the second chorus for SSA chorus. Each of the five settings tell in poetic terms the feelings of a people that drew from Coleridge-Taylor music of great warmth and compassion.

Op. 55 MOORISH DANCE. Composed 1904; published in 1904 by Augener. Pianoforte solo. A delicate and charming piano solo.

Op. 56 CAMEOS. Written in 1904; published in 1904 by Augener. Solos for pianoforte. In three movements: 1. F Major (Allegro ma no troppo), 2. D Minor (Allegro moderato), 3. G Minor (Andante). 17 pp.

Op. 57 SIX SORROW SONGS. Written in 1904; published in 1904 by Augener. Written for voice and pianoforte. Six songs: 1. Oh, What Comes Over the Sea, 2. When I Am Dead My Dearest, 3. Oh, Roses For the Flush of Youth, 4. She Sat and Sang Away, 5. Unmindful of the Roses, 6. Too Late for Love. They were first performed on May 18, 1904, at the

Public Hall, Croydon, by Marie Brema in an all
Coleridge-Taylor recital. They are dedicated to his
wife. The lyrics are by Christina Rossetti. These
are among the most introspective and poignantly
beautiful settings of songs by the composer.

Op. 58 FOUR AFRICAN DANCES. Written in 1902; published in 1904 by Augener, with bowing and fingering by W. Henley. Written for violin and pianoforte.
In four movements: 1. G Minor, 2. F Major, 3. A
Major, 4. D Minor. First performed in 1902 (?)
for the Rochester (England) Choral Society, by
Goldie Baker, violinist with the composer at the
piano.

Op. 59, No. 1. TWENTY-FOUR NEGRO MELODIES. Written in 1904, published in 1905 by Oliver Ditson Co.
Solos for pianoforte of Negro melodies: 1. At the
Dawn of the Day, 2. The Stones Are Very Hard,
3. Take Nabandji, 4. They Will Not Lend Me a
Child, 5. Song of Conquest, 6. Warriors' Song,
7. Oloba, 8. The Bamboula, 9. The Angels Changed
My Name, 10. Deep River, 11. Didn't My Lord Deliver Daniel, 12. Don't Be Weary, 13. Going Up,
14. I'm Troubled in Mind, 15. I Was Way Down A-
Yonder, 16. Let Us Cheer the Weary Traveller,
17. Many Thousand Gone; 18. My Lord Delivered
Daniel; 19. Oh, He Raise a Poor Lazarus, 20. Pilgrim's Song, 21. Run, Mary, Run, 22. Sometimes I
Feel Like a Motherless Child, 23. Steal Away,
24. Wade in the Water. During his first visit to America in 1904, Coleridge-Taylor received an invitation from
the Oliver Ditson Co., Boston, to arrange an album

of Negro folk songs for the piano. He played three
of these arrangements himself in The Music Hall,
Chicago, in 1904. The large audience heard a program consisting entirely of his shorter compositions.
He accompanied Miss Mary Peck Thomson, Theodore Spiering and his dear friend, Harry T. Burleigh, and also played the three solos from his
forthcoming Ditson commission. These were listed
as Three Negro Melodies Symphonically Arranged
from Set of Twenty-Four. The completed work was
published by Ditson in 1905 as Twenty-Four Negro
Melodies. Coleridge-Taylor sent a copy of this
work to Stanford and received the following interesting acknowledgment, dated May 16, 1905.

"My dear Coleridge-Taylor,
'It is very good of you to send me the melo-
dies. They look most characteristic and inte-
resting. I wish you would send a copy to Percy
Grainger, who is greatly interested in folk-songs.
By the way, one of the tunes, The Angel's
Changed My Name, is an Irish tune, and I also
think The Pilgrim's Song. Like some of the
Negro tunes Dvořák got hold of, these have
reached the American Negroes through the Irish-
Americans. A curious instance of the transmi-
gration of folk songs.
'Yours very sincerely,
C. V. Stanford"

Op. 59, No. 2. ROMANCE. Written in 1905 (?); published
in 1905 (?) by Augener. Written for violin and
pianoforte.

Op. 60 Unknown; title missing.

Op. 61 KUBLA KHAN. Written in 1905; published in 1905
by Houghton and Co. After the closing of this firm,
Novello secured the rights to the music in 1914.

Rhapsody for mezzo-soprano solo, chorus and orchestra. First performed by the Handel Society,
Queen's Hall, 1906. The text is by Samuel Taylor
Coleridge. This was the first major choral work in
which the composer used a text by the poet after
whom he was named. In 1905 he met Ernest Hart-
ley Coleridge, grand-nephew of the poet. After tea,
Mr. Coleridge read the composer a lyrical fragment
of "Kubla Khan," and suggested that a musical composition be developed. The mysticism of the poet's
dream appealed to Taylor. The result can be classed
as one of his most evocative and atmospheric works.

Op. 62 INCIDENTAL MUSIC TO NERO. Written in 1906,
published in 1907 by Novello. For orchestra:
2222/4231/timp. perc./hp. str. The Entr'acte,
Intermezzo (Singing Girls' Chorus), Eastern Dance,
Processional March. First performed in 1906 in a
Beerbohm Tree production to a text by Stephen
Phillips at His Majesty's Theatre, London, and dedicated to Tree. Coleridge-Taylor was asked how he
went about setting music for the theater. Sayers recalls his answer: "How does one begin? Well,
first one goes to hear the play read through to get
hold of what the painters call the right atmosphere.
Then the ideas begin to come. And curiously
enough, though Mr. Tree may not be a musician--
that is, from the technical point of view--yet he
always makes one understand exactly what he wants."
Coleridge-Taylor liked the idea of his music being
played so well, so often. 24:00.

Op. 63 SYMPHONIC VARIATIONS ON AN AFRICAN AIR.
Written in 1906; published in 1906 by Novello. Written for orchestra: 3222/4231/timp. perc. /str.
First performed June 14, 1906, at the Philharmonic
Society's Concert, Queen's Hall. The principal
theme (air) is "I'm Troubled in Mind," a song that
was featured by the (Fisk) Jubilee Singers. 20:00.
This unjustly neglected work consists of 14 variations of great ingenuity. Herbert Antcliffe remarked
"We witness the piquant individuality of the man, his
geniality and sentimental but virile tenderness, his
racial fondness for strong rhythmic accents and his
natural conservatism and regard for classic tradition."

Op. 64 SCÈNES DE BALLET. Written in 1906; published
in 1906 by Augener. Solos for pianoforte in four
movements: 1. C Major, 2. A Major, 3. A-Flat
Major, 4. B-Flat Major.

Op. 65 ENDYMION'S DREAM. Written in 1909; published
in 1910 by Novello. A one-act opera for soprano
and tenor soli, chorus and orchestra. First performed February 4, 1910, at the Brighton Music
Festival. Text by C. R. B. Barrett and based on
the work by John Keats. It is the story of the
Hellenic priest, Endymion, who is granted immor-
tality, but with the addition of eternal sleep. He is
loved by the moon, Selene. Selene awakens Endymion in a cave on Mount Latmos. There is a mutual
surrender and a "Cataclysm that results from Selene's deviation from her appointed course." After
the Brighton performance, Coleridge-Taylor rewrote

the choruses from female to mixed voices. Beerbohm Tree was interested, and had it presented as
a production at His Majesty's Theatre. Taylor was
particularly fond of the tenor solo, "Who Calls,"
from Endymion's Dream and felt it was a finer work
than "Onaway, Awake" from Hiawatha.

Op. 66 FOREST SCENES. Written in 1907; published in
1907 by Augener. Five characteristic pieces for
pianoforte solo in five movements: 1. A Minor,
The Love Forest Maiden, 2. E-Flat Major, The
Phantom Lover Arrives, 3. E Major, The Phantom
Tells His Tale of Longing, 4. E Major, Erstwhile
They Ride; The Forest Maiden Acknowledges Her
Love, 5. C Major, Now Proudly They Journey To-
gether Towards the Great City.

Op. 67 PART-SONGS (S. A. T. B.). Written in 1905; published in 1905 by Augener. Three choral settings
in three movements: 1. All My Stars Forsake Me,
2. Dead in the Sierras (lyrics by Joaquin Miller
from Poems of Wild Life in the Canterbury Poets),
3. The Fair of Almachara (lyrics by R. H. Horne).

Op. 68 BON-BON SUITE. Written in 1908; published in
1908 by Novello. A cantata for baritone solo, chorus and orchestra in six movements: 1. The Magic
Mirror, 2. The Fairy Boat, 3. To Rosa, 4. Love
and Hymen, 5. The Watchman, 6. Say What Shall
We Dance. First performed on January 14, 1909,
at the Brighton Musical Festival, Coleridge-Taylor
conductor, with one of his favorite singers, Henry
Julien, as soloist. Dedicated to Miss Sunshine
(Doris). The dedication recalls his love of children.

During a holiday at Worthing one summer, Coleridge-
Taylor developed a friendship with seven-year-old
Doris Sunshine, and this was the Miss Sunshine referred to in the dedication. The text is by Thomas
Moore. The title caused problems and misconcep-
tions. Finally Taylor issued a small prospectus saying, "It has been deemed advisable to point out that
this suite is not orchestral, but choral ... and is in
every way like a cantata, excepting that it is divided
into six short numbers." Vocal score: 79 pp.

Op. 69 SEA-DRIFT. Written in 1908; published in 1908 by
Novello. Rhapsody for unaccompanied 8-part chorus.
Text by Walt Whitman   18 pp.

Op. 70 INCIDENTAL MUSIC TO FAUST. Written in 1908,
published in 1908 as a pianoforte version, and in
1909 in orchestral form by Boosey. Written for orchestra. The incidental music included: Dance of
Witches (Brocken Scene), 2:30; The Four Visions--
Helen, 2:30; Cleopatra, 2:00; Messalina, 1:30;
Margaret, 3:00; Dance and Chant (Devil's Kitchen
Scene), 3:30. Also the song, "A King There Lived
in Thule." Written for the Beerbohm Tree production to Stephen Phillips' and J. Comyn Carr's version of Goethe's drama, which opened at His Majesty's Theatre, September 7, 1908. Coleridge-
Taylor was concerned about comparisons to Gounod
and Berlioz.

Not all the music for the production was by
Coleridge-Taylor. The production included the Berlioz Minuet des Folles and Ballet des Sylphes.

Op. 71 THREE FOURS VALSE SUITE. Written in 1908-9; published in 1909 by Augener. Solos for pianoforte in six movements: 1. A Minor (Allegro molto), 2. A-Flat Major (Andante), 3. G Minor (Allegro moderato), 4. D Major (Vivace), 5. E-Flat Major (Andante molto), 6. C Minor (Allegro assai). Dedicated to Miss Myrtle Meggy. 18:30. 23 pp.

Op. 72 THELMA. Written in 1906-08 (ms.)--probably published in 1908 by Ascherberg-Hawkes. A grand opera in three acts. The opera was never performed. However the Prelude to Thelma was played in March 1910 by the New London Symphony Orchestra (London, England). Thelma was a poetical setting of a Norwegian saga-legend put into modern terms. Coleridge-Taylor was very much in love with the theater and opera and had always hoped for an operatic production. He felt that the famous Carl Rosa Opera Company would find Thelma suitable. Although the opera director found merit in the music, the libretto and stage theatricality were hopelessly inadequate and the opera was never accepted for production.

Op. 73 BALLADE IN C MINOR. Written in 1907; published in 1909 by Augener. Written for violin and pianoforte in five movements: 1. Molto moderato, 2. Allegro, 3. Più andante e tranquillo, 4. Allegro vivace, 5. L'istesso tempo. First performed October 29, 1907, at Leeds by Zacharewitsch, violinist, with Coleridge-Taylor at the piano.

Op. 73a PART SONGS (TTBB). Written in 1909; published in 1910 by Curwen, in four movements: 1. Are

All Sleeping, Weary Heart (Henry Wadsworth Longfellow), 2. Loud Sang the Spanish Cavalier (Longfellow), 3. O Mariners, Out of the Sunlight (Robert
Buchanan), 4. O, Who Will Worship the Great God
Pan.

Op. 74 INCIDENTAL MUSIC TO THE FOREST OF WILD
THYME. Written in 1910-1911; published in 1911 by
Boosey. Written for full orchestra and female
voices. The music is essentially in five movements:
1. Scenes from an Imaginary Ballet (which is itself
in five sections: (a) D Major, Molto vivace; (b) B-
flat Major, Allegretto; (c) G Major, Tempo di menu-
etto; (d) A-flat Major, Andantino; (e) A Minor, Vi-
vacissimo); 2. Three Dream Dances ((a) D Major;
(b) F Major; (c) G Major); 3. Intermezzo; 4. Vocal music ((a) Your Heart's Desire; (b) Little Boy
Blue; (c) Come In; (d) Dreams, Dreams); 5 Christmas Overture, 5:00. Play never performed. "The
Forest of Wild Thyme" was commissioned by Beerbohm Tree to a poetical fairy tale by Alfred Noyes.
Ultimately it was abandoned, probably because of a
similarity to the contemporary "Blue-Bird" of
Maeterlinck. The Christmas Overture was a popular section and enjoyed many performances.

Op. 75 THE BAMBOULA. Written in 1910, published in
1911 by Hawkes. A Rhapsodic Dance for orchestra:
3222/4231/timp. B. drum, side drum, cym., tri./
str. First performed at the Norfolk, Conn. Musical Festival, 1911. Dedicated to Mr. and Mrs.
Carl Stoeckel. 9:00. The Bamboula is a West Indian dance and formed the groundwork of this

orchestral rhapsody. It could have the same popular appeal that Scott Joplin rags presently enjoy.
Coleridge-Taylor brought the score and parts with
him when he came to the United States in May 1910.
It was a popular triumph. The composer-conductor
was delighted with the superb orchestra that could
perfect it in only two rehearsals. The front cover
for the set of parts to The Bamboula has the following program notes by Taylor: "This work was first
played by the New York Philharmonic Orchestra in
June, 1910, and was the result of a suggestion from
Mr. Carl Stoeckel, to whom the work is inscribed.
The four bars beginning with the letter B are identi-
cal with a well known West Indies Negro dance
called 'The Bamboula,' the tempo of the original
Bamboula being quite fast throughout. No other subject matter is used through-out the composition,
which is merely a series of evolutions of the phrase
mentioned. This refers to the middle part also,
which is introduced for the sake of contrast. "

Op. 76 A TALE OF OLD JAPAN. Composed in 1911; published in 1911 by Novello. A cantata for soprano,
contralto, tenor and baritone soli, chorus and orchestra. First performed by the London Choral Society, conducted by Arthur Fagge, in Queen's Hall,
London, December 6, 1911. Dedication "To Mr.
and Mrs. Carl Stoeckel, with happiest remembrances
of the White House, Norfolk, Conn. U.S.A., and
the people I met there. " Early in 1910, the composer was introduced to the works of Alfred Noyes.
He was immediately attracted to the singability of

his lyrics. 48:00. There is an interesting observation in his wife's 1943 book. She says that her husband preferred "A Tale" to Hiawatha. Also, he was bitterly disappointed that he was not asked to conduct its first performance. But also, he had to pay for four tickets (for himself, his wife and two guests) to hear his own world premiere!

The story relates how Yoichi Tenko, the painter, was the guardian of little O Kimi San, the orphan child of his brother. A student, Sawara, came to study at the painter's school. He showed such ability that he was told he could learn no more from the school of Tenka, and must seek inspiration and fortune elsewhere. Then it appeared that O Kimi San and Sawara were lovers. The young artist was told to achieve a career before he could be united to Kimi. The lovers parted with a hope of soon meeting again. Tenko, however, had other plans for Kimi. He falsely said that Sawara was unfaithful and induced her to marry a rich young merchant with "bags of gold." After achieving fame, Sawara returns to the school of Tenko, and finds that Kimi is married. Later, he meets Kimi, who still feels love for him. When she finds that he is cold to her, "Trembling, she lifted her head / Then like a broken blossom / It fell on her arm. She was dead."

Op. 77 PETITE SUITE DE CONCERT. Written in 1911, published in 1911 by Hawkes. For full orchestra: 3222/4230/timp. drums/str. In four movements:
1. Le Caprice de Nanette (Allegro con brio),
2. Demande et Reponse (Andante), 3. Un Sonnet

d'Amour (Allegretto), 4. La Tarantelle Fretillante
(Vivace). 14:30 (4:00, 4:30, 3:30, 2:30).

Op. 78 THREE IMPROMPTUS. Written in 1911; published
in 1911 by Weekes. Solos for organ in three movements: 1. F Major, 2. C Major, 3. A Minor.
12:00.

Op. 79 INCIDENTAL MUSIC TO OTHELLO. Written in
1911; published in 1911 by Metzler. Written for orchestra: 3222/4221/timp. perc. /str. First performed at Her Majesty's Theatre. Dedicated to
Miss Phyllis Neilson-Terry. The play was Shakespeare. 11:30. Coleridge-Taylor developed five
sections into an orchestral suite: The Dance,
Children's Intermezzo, Funeral March, The Willow
Song, Military March.

Coleridge-Taylor was full of enthusiasm for
Shakespeare and the Beerbohm Tree production.

Op. 80 CONCERTO IN G MINOR. Written in 1911; published in 1912 by Metzler. Concerto for violin and
orchestra. First performed at the Norfolk, Conn.
Musical Festival, 1911. Dedicated to Maud Powell,
the American violinist. The concerto is considered
one of Coleridge-Taylor's finest works. It was actually first played by William I. Read, the violinist
friend of the composer in the Small Public Hall,
Croydon, for friends. Read proofread the concerto
and both edited and indicated tempo markings as he
recalled them from the composer. The following
inscription is found on the score: "The publishers
are indebted to Mr. William J. Read for kindly
reading the proofs and editing this work. The

metronome marks are in accordance with the tempi
edited by the composer when the concerto was
played by Mr. Read and accompanied by Mr. Coleridge-Taylor himself. This was the only occasion
upon which the composer was personally associated
with a performance of the work." There were two
versions of the concerto. The first version was
built on Negro melodies, but these Coleridge-Taylor
finally rejected as placing limitations on his con-
ception of the work.

Carl Stoeckel had suggested that Coleridge-Taylor
incorporate Negro melodies in each movement. The
original version utilized one spiritual, "Many Thousands Gone," in the second movement and "Yankee-
Doodle" in the third, which, of course, is not a black
melody.

Op. 81 TWO SONGS. Written in 1912; published in 1920 by
Boosey. Written with orchestral or pianoforte ac-
companiment in two movements; 1. Waiting and 2.
Red O'the Dawn. Lyrics by Alfred Noyes.

Op. 82, No. 1. HIAWATHA BALLET MUSIC. Published by
Hawkes. This is musically unconnected from the
three Hiawatha cantatas. They were arranged and
orchestrated after the composer's death by Percy E.
Fletcher for full orchestra. In five sections:
1. The Wooing, 2. The Marriage Feast, 3. Bird
Scene and Conjurer's Dance, 4. The Departure,
5. Reunion. 18:00 (7:00; 3:30; 1:30; 4:00; 2:00). It
is interesting to note that Coleridge-Taylor was
fascinated with the Hiawatha theme until the end of

his life. Both ballets (op. 82, 1 and 2) were completed by August 1912 but not the scoring.

Op. 82, No. 2. MINNEHAHA BALLET MUSIC. Published
by Hawkes. This is also musically unconnected to
the cantata, The Death of Minnehaha. It was also
arranged and orchestrated after the composer's
death by Percy E. Fletcher for full orchestra. In
four sections: 1. Laughing Water, 2. The Pursuit,
3. Love Song, 4. The Homecoming. 19:30.

2. THE LISTING OF NON-OPUS-NUMBER WORKS

Accompaniments to Poems (ms.)

Clown and Columbine
The Parting Glass

Anthems

Break Forth into Joy. Pub. 1892, Novello
By the Waters of Babylon. 1899, Novello
In Thee, O Lord, Have I Put My Trust. 1891, Novello
Lift Up Your Heads. 1892, Novello
Now Late on the Sabbath Day. 1901, Novello
O Ye That Love the Lord. 1892, Novello
The Lord Is My Strength. 1892, Novello
What Thou Has Given Me. 1901(?), Weekes

Choir and Organ

Te Deum in F Major. A Simple Setting for Parish Choirs.
Composed in 1890 and later published as part of op. 18.

Duet

Keep Those Eyes. Soprano and Tenor. 1903, Novello.
Text: Thomas Moore.

Hymn Tune

Luconor. "Jesu, the Very Thought of Thee. " Methodist
Sunday School Hymnal.

Orchestra

From the Prairie, Rhapsody. Composed for and performed
at the Norfolk, Conn. Music Festival, 1914. Pub.
Hawkes.
Re-orchestration of the accompaniments to Ernst's Violin
Concerto in F Minor (ms.).
Trio in E Minor (ms.).
Deep River (ms.). 5:30
I'm Troubled in Mind (ms.). 5:30

Incidental Music to St. Agnes Eve

Written in 1910 for full orchestra. In three movements:
1. That Ancient Beadsman Heard the Prelude of Soft,
2. Her Maiden Eyes Divine, 3. Porphyro, Now Tell Us
Where Is Madelin! Published by Hawkes. 8:00 (3:00;
2:00; 3:00). This was a musical accompaniment for
the Keats Story and was produced on June 10, 1910, at
the Keats-Shelley Festival in London.

Salon Orchestra

A Lovely Little Dream. Strings and harmonium in Vol. 2
of "De Groot and the Picadilly Orchestra Series. "
Pub. Metzler

Organ

Three Short Pieces, published in 1898 by Novello. 1. Melody, 2:30, 2. Elegy, 2:30, 3. Arietta, 3:00. The
theme for this melody is taken from the fourth version
of Coleridge-Taylor's unpublished Symphony, op. 8
(fourth movement). The three organ solos were published as part of Novello's The Village Organist (Books
12, 15, 16).

Part Songs (S. A.)

Beauty and Truth. Pub. Curwen
Drake's Drum. Text: Henry Newboldt. Pub. Curwen.
2:45

Fall On Me Like a Silent Dew from Othello music. Text:
   Robert Herrick. Pub. Curwen
Oh! The Summer. Text: Isabel Ecclestone Mackay. Pub.
   Curwen
Viking Song. Text: David McKee Wright. Pub. Curwen.
   2:30

Part Songs (S. S. A.)

A June Rose Bloomed. Text: Louise Alston Burleigh. Pub.
   1906, Augener
Encinctured with a Twine of Leaves. Text: Samuel Coleridge-
   Taylor. Pub. 1908, Novello
The Pixies. Text: Samuel Coleridge-Taylor. Pub. 1908,
   Novello
What Can Lambkins Do. Text: Christina Rossetti. Pub.
   1908, Novello

Part Songs (S. A. T. B.)

By the Lone Seashore. Text: Charles Mackay. Pub. 1910,
   Novello. 3:10
The Evening Star. Text: Thomas Campbell. Pub. 1911,
   Novello. 2:20
Isle of Beauty. Text: T. H. Bayly (1797-1839). Pub.
   1920, Augener
The Lee Shore. Text: Thomas Hood. Pub. 1912, Novello.
   2:50
The Sea-Shell. Text: Tennyson. Pub. 1911, Curwen
Song of the Prosperpine. Text: Shelley. Pub. 1912, No-
   vello
Summer Is Gone. Text: Christina Rossetti. 3:00
Whispers of Summer. Pub. in Musical Times, Vol. #51
   (1910), p. 810

Unison Chorus

Prayer for Peace. Text: Alfred Noyes. Written in April,
   1911

Pianoforte Solo

Papillon. Pub. 1908, Augener
Two Impromptus: 1. A Major, 2. B Minor. Pub. 1911,
   Augener
Two Oriental Waltzes: 1. Haidee, 2. Zuleika. Pub.
   Forsyth

Songs

A Birthday. Text: Christina Rossetti. Pub. Metzler, 1910
A Corn Song. Text: Dunbar. Pub. Boosey, 1897
A Dance of Bygone Days (ms.)
Oh, Sweet, Thou Little Knowest. Pub. Ricordi
Oh Tell Me Gentle Zephyr (ms.)
A Lament. Text: Christina Rossetti. Pub. Ricordi, 1910.
    2:45
A Lovely Little Dream. Text: Sarojini Naidu. Pub. Metz-
    ler, 1909
An Explanation. Pub. Augener, 1914
A Summer Idyll. Text: Helda Hammond-Spencer. Pub.
    Enoch, 1906
A Vengeance (ms.). This was one of the few songs to be
    refused by publishers because they felt "the words
    were too strong. "
A Vision. Text: Louise Alston Burleigh. Pub. Presser,
    1905
Candle Lightin' Time. Text: Dunbar. Pub. John Church
    (Ditson), 1911
Dimple-Chin (ms.)
Eulalie. Text: Alice Parsons. Pub. Boosey, 1904
Five Fairy Ballads: Sweet Baby Butterfly, Alone with
    Mother, Big Lady Moon, The Stars, Fairy Roses.
    Text: Kathleen Easmon. Pub. Boosey, 1909. Eas-
    mon was a young West African girl whom Coleridge-
    Taylor felt had great talent.
Five and Twenty Sailormen. Text: Greville E. Matheson.
    Pub. John Church Co. , 1910. 3:00
Genevieve. Text: S. T. Coleridge [the poet]. Presser, 1905
If I Could Love Thee. Text: Louise Alston Burleigh. Pub.
    Presser, 1905
Life and Death. Pub. Augener, 1914. 1:45
Love's Mirror. Song for Michelmas Day. Written in 1897
Love's Passing. Text: Louise Alston Burleigh
Love's Questionings. Text: Alice Parsons. Pub. Keith,
    Browse and Co. , 1904
Low Breathing Winds. Pub. Augener, 1914
My Algonquin. Text: Longfellow. Pub. Presser, 1909
O Mistress Mine. Text: Shakespeare. Pub. Rogers, 1906
Once Only. Text: Robert Louis Stevenson. Pub. Rogers,
    1906
Our Idyll. Text: Adriene Ross (after the part song, "A
    June Rose Bloomed"). Pub. Augener, 1906
Prithee, Tell Me (ms.)
She Rested by the Broken Brook. Text: Robert Lewis

Stevenson, from <u>Praise and Ballads</u>. Pub. Rogers. 3:00

Solitude. Text: Lord Byron. Written and performed in 1893; Coleridge-Taylor's earliest known song. Pub. Augener, 1918

Song of the Nubian Girl. Text: Thomas Moore. Pub. Augener, 1905

Songs of Sun and Shade: 1. You Lay So Still in the Sunshine, 2. Thou Hast Bewitched Me, Beloved, 3. The Rainbow Child, 4. Thou Art Risen, My Beloved, 5. This Is the Island of Gardens. Text: Margaret Radcliffe-Hall. Pub. Boosey, 1911

Sons of the Sea. Text: Sarojini Naidu. Pub. Novello, 1911. 3:15

Tell, O Tell Me. Pub. Augener, 1914

The Arrow and the Song (ms.)

The Broken Oar (ms.)

The Delaware's Farewell (ms.)

The Easter Morn (sacred song). Text: Arthur Chapman. Pub. Enoch, 1904

The Gift Rose. Text: Dr. Frederic Peterson. Pub. Rogers, 1907

The Guest (written in 1911). Text: Herrick (1591-1674). Pub. Augener, 1914

The Links o' Love. Text: G. E. Matheson. Pub. John Church Co., 1910

The Oasis. Text: Adrien Ross (after the part song "We Strew These Opiate Flowers"). Pub. Augener, 1898

The Shoshone's Adieu. Text: Brice Fennell. Pub. Boosey, 1904

The Three Ravens. A traditional English air of the six-teenth century with German words by Wilhelmine Grotjohann Dohrn. Pub. Boosey, 1897

The Violet Bank. Text: Darling. Pub. Presser

Thou Art. Pub. Presser

Three Song Poems: 1. Dreaming Forever, 2. The Young Indian Maid, 3. Beauty and Song. Text: Thomas Moore. Enoch 1905

Three Songs of Heine (English and German words): 1. My Pretty Fishermaiden, 2. Thy Sapphire Eyes, 3. I Hear the Flutes and Fiddles. English text: Elizabeth Lockwood. Pub. Augener, 1918

Toujours, l'amour (ms.)

Two Songs: 1. My Lady (lyrics by E. R. Stephenson) and 2. Love's Mirror (lyrics by F. Hart). Pub. Augener, 1916

Until. Text: Frank Dempster Sherman. Pub. Rogers

Viking Song. Arr. by Percy Fletcher. Pub. Curwen
We Watched Her Breaking Through the Night (ms.)
Why Does Azure Deck the Skies? (ms.)
Who Calls? (ms.)

Violin

Slow Movement on a Negro Melody, Deep River (ms.) (with
pianoforte)
Slow Movement on a Negro Melody, Keep Me from Sinking
Down (ms.) (Violin and orchestra.) Written for and
first performed at the Norfolk (Conn.) Music Festival,
1911
Slow Movement on a Negro Melody, Many Thousand Gone
(ms.) (with pianoforte)
Transcription of the Allegretto Grazioso from Dvořák's Symphony in G Major, op. 88 (with pianoforte).

Violoncello

Variations in B Minor for Violoncello and Pianoforte. First
performed November 30, 1907, by Mr. C. A. Crabbe
at the String Players Concert, Croydon. Pub. 1919,
Augener
Fantasiestück in A Major (ms.) (violoncello and orchestra).
First performed July 7, 1907, by Mary McCullagh at
the Tower, New Brighton

3. SELECTED ARRANGEMENTS OF COLERIDGE-TAYLOR'S
WORKS by the Composer and by Others with His Author-
ization (during his lifetime)

Op. 3   SUITE DE PIÈCES. No. 2, Cavatina, and No. 3,
Barcarolle, published as pianoforte solos.

Op. 4   BALLADE IN D MINOR. Arranged for violin and
pianoforte by the composer.

Op. 9   TWO ROMANTIC PIECES. No. 1, Lament, arranged for pianoforte solo.

Op. 14   LEGEND FROM CONCERTSTÜCK. Arranged for
violin and pianoforte.

Op. 20 GIPSY SUITE. No. 3 A Gipsy Dance, arranged for
violoncello and pianoforte.

Op. 22 FOUR CHARACTERISTIC WALTZES. Arranged for
pianoforte solo; violin and pianoforte; and quintet for
pianoforte and strings, by the composer.

Op. 30, No. 3. OVERTURE TO THE SONG OF HIAWATHA.
Arranged for pianoforte solo (1899) by the composer.

Op. 33 BALLADE IN A MINOR. Arranged for pianoforte
solo (1898) by the composer.

Op. 35 AFRICAN SUITE. No. 2 arranged for violin and pianoforte (1898 and 1908), with fingering by J. Henley.
No. 4, arranged for violin and pianoforte (1898);
also for full orchestra (1901).

Op. 38 THREE SILHOUETTES. No. 1 arranged for violin
and pianoforte.

Op. 41, No. 1. SCENES FROM AN EVERYDAY ROMANCE.
Arranged for pianoforte solo by the composer.

Op. 47, No. 1. INCIDENTAL MUSIC TO HEROD. Fourth
movement (Finale) arranged for pianoforte solo and
pianoforte duet.

Op. 47, No. 2. HEMO DANCE. Arranged for violin and
pianoforte.

Op. 51 ETHIOPIA SALUTING THE COLOURS. Arranged
for pianoforte solo (1902) by the composer.

Op. 52 FOUR NOVELLETTEN. Arranged for violin and pianoforte (1903) by the composer.

Op. 59, No. 1. TWENTY-FOUR NEGRO MELODIES. The
composer arranged Nos. 4, 11, 15, 18 and 22 as
trios for violin, violoncello and pianoforte; and Nos.
4, 5, 7, 12, and 14 for orchestra (1906).

Op. 62 INCIDENTAL MUSIC TO NERO. Suite of Four
Pieces: No. 1, Prelude (Second Entr'acte), Poppaea.
No. 1, Intermezzo (Singing Girls' Chorus). No. 3,
Eastern Dance. No. 4, Finale (First Entr'acte).
All arranged for violin and pianoforte by the com-

poser. The suite was also arranged for pianoforte solo by the composer.

Op. 63 SYMPHONIC VARIATIONS ON AN AFRICAN AIR. Arranged for pianoforte solo by the composer (1906).

Op. 70 INCIDENTAL MUSIC TO FAUST. Pianoforte version of the song, "A King There Lived in Thule" (1908).

4. SELECTED ARRANGEMENTS PUBLISHED AFTER COLERIDGE-TAYLOR'S DEATH

Op. 12 SOUTHERN LOVE SONGS. Nos. 3 and 4 appear in a piano album entitled "Melodies," arranged by A. Roloff.

Op. 17 AFRICAN ROMANCES. Nos. 1 and 4, arranged for pianoforte solo by A. Roloff, were published in an album entitled "Lyrics."

Op. 19, No. 1. MOORISH TONE-PICTURES. "Zarifa," the second movement, was published in simplified form for pianoforte solo in the "Melodies" album, arranged by A. Roloff.

Op. 21 PART SONGS. Nos. 1 and 2 were arranged for pianoforte solo by A. Roloff in the "Melodies." They were given new titles: "From the East" and "Idyll."

Op. 26 THE GITANOS. A. Roloff arranged "Isola" from this operetta for pianoforte solo.

Op. 29 THREE SONGS. The third movement, "Jessy," was arranged for pianoforte solo by A. Roloff and appeared in an album entitled "Lyrics."

Op. 30, No. 1. HIAWATHA'S WEDDING FEAST. This entire cantata appeared as an organ solo in 1920 in an arrangement by Hugh Blair.

Op. 57 SORROW SONGS. Cedric Sharpe arranged string quartet accompaniment to the songs. No. 2 appears

under the title "Reflection" in the Melodies Album
by A. Roloff, but under the title "Regret" in the album of Six Easy Pieces by B. Constance Hull.

Op. 58 FOUR AFRICAN DANCES. A. Roloff arranged nos.
2 and 4 as pianoforte solos. They were published
as "Two African Idyls. "

Op. 59, No. 1. TWENTY-FOUR NEGRO MELODIES. Maud
Powell, the American violinist, arranged "Deep
River" as a violin solo with pianoforte accompani-
ment.

Op. 67 PART SONGS. The "Melodies" album by A. Roloff
includes the second movement as a pianoforte solo.
It appears under the new title, "In the Sierras. "

Op. 77 PETITE SUITE DE CONCERT. Cedric Sharpe arranged no. 2 for violoncello and pianoforte.

Op. 80 CONCERTO IN G MINOR. Published in an edition
for violin and pianoforte (1912) by J. Read.

5. COLERIDGE-TAYLOR WORKS CURRENTLY AVAILABLE
IN PUBLISHERS' CATALOGS

Sacred Choral Music

By the Waters of Babylon. Lenten Anthem, SATB and organ.
Pub. Novello, # 28. 0644. 04
Lift Up Your Heads. Festival Anthem, SATB and organ.
Pub. Novello, # 28. 0409. 03. Also Gray, # GCMR 1460.
O Ye That Love the Lord. Lenten Anthem, SATB and organ.
Pub. Novello, # 40. 0882. 00
The Lord Is My Strength. Easter Anthem, SATB and organ.
Pub. Novello, # 28. 0398. 04

Secular Choral Music

Bon Bon Suite, op. 68. Baritone solo, chorus, piano (vocal
score). Originally with orchestra. Pub. Novello.
Fall on Me Like a Silent Dew. Two-part anthem for junior
choir or women's voices. Pub. Curwen # 71376.

From the Green Heart of the Waters. For SSA. Pub. Novello # 51. 0345. 02.
Hiawatha's Wedding Feast. For SATB chorus, tenor solo,
piano. Pub. G. Schirmer. Also Novello # 07. 007700
for SSAA, piano (arr. H. A. Chambers).
The Lee Shore. SATB, a cappella. Pub. Novello
45. 1231. 06.
O Mariner, Out of the Sunlight. Men's chorus. Pub. Curwen # 50462.
Oh, the Summer. Two-part chorus for junior choir or women's voices. Pub. Curwen # 71308.
Viking Song. Two-part chorus for junior choir or women's
voices. Pub. Curwen # 1307. Also for SATB, Curwen
60982; unison voices (arr. Jacobson). Curwen
72564.

Piano Solo

Waltzes for Piano (Valse de la Reine; Valse Mauresque;
Valse Rustique; Valse Bohémienne; no. 2 from Three
Dream Dances; no. 6 from Three Fours). Pub. Willis,
Cincinnati
Four Characteristic Waltzes. Pub. Novello
24 Negro Melodies. Pub. Oliver Ditson Co.

Orchestra (Rental Only)

Ballade in A Minor, op. 33. Luck's Music Rental, Detroit,
932.
The Bamboula, Rhapsodic Dance. Luck's # 5299.
Christmas Overture. Luck's # 5300.
Danse Nègre, op. 35, no. 4. Luck's # 5302.
Death of Minnehaha, op. 30, no. 2. For soprano, baritone
soloists, SATB chorus, orchestra. Novello and Luck's
7617.
Eastern Dance. For orchestra. Novello.
First Entr'acte, from Nero. For orchestra. Novello.
Four Characteristic Waltzes, op. 22. For orchestra. No-
vello and Luck's # 9133.
Hiawatha's Departure, op. 30, no. 4. For soprano, bari-
tone soloists, SATB chorus, orchestra. Novello and
Luck's # 7618.
Hiawatha's Wedding Feast, op. 30, no. 1. For tenor solo-
ist, SATB chorus, orchestra. Novello and Luck's
7616.
Hiawatha: Suite, from the Ballet. Luck's # 8933.
Novelletten, op. 52, no. 1. For string orchestra. Novello.

Novelletten, op. 52, no. 2. For string orchestra. Novello.
Novelletten, op. 52, no. 3. For string orchestra. Novello.
Novelletten, op. 52, no. 4. For string orchestra. Novello.
Onaway! Awake Beloved, from op. 30. Tenor solo.
Luck's #2823.
Petite Suite de Concert. Luck's # 7619.
Scenes from an Imaginary Ballet. Luck's # 5301.
Second Entr'acte, from Negro. For orchestra. Novello.
Suite from Nero. For orchestra. Novello.
Viking Song. For male chorus and orchestra. Luck's
3044.

Organ

Willow Song from Othello. Arr. for organ by Frank E.
Brown. Pub. J. B. Cramer, London.

Appendix B

A LISTING OF COLERIDGE-TAYLOR'S MUSIC BY CATEGORY

Operas

Op.	25	Dream Lovers	72	Thelma
	26	The Gitanos		

Incidental Music to Plays

Op.	47	Herod	70	Faust
	49	Ulysses	79	Othello
	62	Nero		

Choral Music

Op.	15	Land of the Sun		Castel-Cuillé
	21	Two Part Songs	48	Meg Blane
	30	Song of Hiawatha	53	The Atonement
		1. Hiawatha's Wedding Feast	54	Five Choral Ballads
			61	Kubla Khan
		2. The Death of Minnehaha	65	Endymion's Dream
			67	Three Part Songs
		3. Hiawatha's Departure	68	Bon-Bon Suite
			69	Sea-Drift
	35ii	How They So Softly Rest	73a	Four Part Songs
			76	A Tale of Old Japan
	43	The Blind Girl of		

also various choral pieces without opus number

Orchestral Music

Op.	8	Symphony in A Minor	30iii	Overture to The Song of Hiawatha
	22	Four Characteristic Waltzes	31	Three Humoresques
			33	Ballade in A Minor

Op.					
35	African Suite		52	Four Novelletten	
40	A Solemn Prelude		63	Symphonic Variations on	
41i	Scenes from an			an African Air	
	Everyday Romance		74iii	Intermezzo, Forest of	
41ii	Nourmahal's Song			Wild Thyme	
	and Dance		74v	Christmas Overture,	
44	Idyll			Forest of Wild Thyme	
46	Toussaint L'Ouver-		75	The Bamboula	
	ture		77	Petite Suite de Con-	
47ii	Hemo Dance			cert	
51	Ethiopia Saluting		82i	Hiawatha Ballet Music	
	the Colours		82ii	Minnehaha Ballet Music	

Violin and Orchestra

Op. 4 Ballade in D Minor 39 Romance in G Major
14 Legend from the 80 Concerto in G Minor
Concertstück

Voice and Orchestra

Op. 7 Zara's Earrings 42 The Soul's Expression
81 Two Songs

Chamber Music

Op. 1 Quintet in G Minor 10 Quintet in A Major
2 Nonet in F Minor 13 String Quartet
5 Fantasiestücke

Violin and Pianoforte

Op. 3 Suite de Pieces 23 Valse Caprice
9 Two Romantic 28 Sonata in D Minor
Pieces 58 Four African Dances
16 Hiawatha Sketches 59ii Romance
20 Gipsy Suite 73 Ballade in C Minor

Pianoforte Music

Op. 19i Two Moorish Tone 56 Cameos
Pictures 59i Twenty Four Negro
22 Four Character- Melodies
istic Waltzes 64 Scenes de Ballet
31 Three Humoresques 66 Forest Scenes
38 Three Silhouettes 71 Three Fours Valse
55 Moorish Dances Suite

Op. 74i   Scenes From an Imaginary Ballet

Organ Music

Op. 78   Three Impromptus
          also some music without opus number

Songs with Pianoforte

12	Southern Love	29	Three Songs
	Songs	37	Six Songs
17	African Romances	45	Six American Lyrics
19ii	Little Songs for	50	Three Song-Poems
	Little Folks	57	Six Sorrow Songs
24	In Memoriam		

also many songs without opus number

Church Music

Op. 18   Morning and Eve-   -- Lift Up Your Heads
          ning Service in F   -- Now Late on the Sabbath
          Major   Day
      -- In Thee O Lord   -- O Ye That Serve the Lord
      -- By the Waters of   -- The Lord Is My Strength
          Babylon   -- What Thou Has Given Me
      -- Break Forth into Joy

Appendix C

A LISTING OF MUSIC IN ALPHABETICAL ORDER

African Dances, Four (op. 58)

African Romances (op. 17)

African Suite (op. 35)

American Lyrics, Six (op. 45)

The Atonement (op. 53)

Ballade in A Minor (op. 33)

Ballade in C Minor (op. 73)

Ballade in D Minor (op. 4)

The Bamboula (op. 75)

The Blind Girl of Castel-
Cuillé (op. 43)

Bon-Bon Suite (op. 68)

Cameos (op. 56)

Characteristic Waltzes, Four
(op. 22)

Choral Ballads, Five (op. 54)

Concerto in G Minor (op. 80)

The Death of Minnehaha (op.
30, no. 2)

Dream Lovers (op. 25)

Endymion's Dream (op. 65)

Ethiopia Saluting the Colours
(op. 51)

Fantasiestücke (op. 5)

Faust, Incidental Music to
(op. 70)

Forest of Wild Thyme, In-
cidental Music to the (op.
74)

Forest Scenes (op. 66)

Gipsy Suite (op. 20)

The Gitanos (op. 26)

Hemo Dance (op. 47, no. 2)

Herod, Incidental Music to
(op. 47, no. 1)

Hiawatha Ballet Music (op.
82, no. 1)

Hiawathan Sketches (op. 16)

Hiawatha's Departure (op.
30, no. 4)

Hiawatha's Wedding Feast
(op. 30, no. 1)

How They So Softly Rest
(op. 35, no. 2)

Humoresques, Three (op.
31)

Idyll (op. 44)

Impromptus, Three (op. 78)

In Memoriam (op. 24)

Appendix D

A DISCOGRAPHY OF COLERIDGE-TAYLOR

There is very little music by Coleridge-Taylor available on recordings. The following list includes music by the composer that was circulated commercially. They are no longer in circulation and difficult to find except through discovery at a record collectors shop.

The Institute of Recorded Sound, Exhibition Road, London has five selections on tape which are available for listening on appointment.

In addition, two recordings are presently available commercially. Hiawatha's Wedding Feast, Sir Malcolm Sargent conducting the Royal Choral Society and Philharmonic Orchestra with Richard Lewis, Tenor, is available in England (EMI-ASD 467). Also of interest are Danse Nègre, and "Onaway! Awake, Beloved" from Hiawatha's Wedding Feast. These two compositions are available in the United States as part of the Columbia Records Series, Black Composers. It is performed by the London Symphony, Paul Freeman, Conductor, and William Brown, Tenor (COL M32782).

The following list does not include private recordings.

ORCHESTRAL-CHORAL

1. Christmas Overture, op. 74, no. 5, from incidental
   music to the play, The Forest of Wild Thyme (pre-
   1936 recording). BBC Orchestra, cond. Pitt (C.
   9137).

2. The Death of Minnehaha (pre-1936 recording). Royal
   Choral Society, cond. Sargent (GC 2210/3).

3. Faust, Incidental Music, op. 70, no. 1, Dance of the
   Witches, and no. 3, Devil's Kitchen. Regent Concert
   Orchestra (BH 1922).

4. Four Characteristic Waltzes, op. 22 (pre-1936 recording). New Light Symphony Orchestra, cond. Murray
   (GB 8378 and Vic. 27225/6).

5. Hiawatha, Concert Suite, op. 82, no. 1. Conjurers'
   Dance, arranged and orchestrated by P. Fletcher.
   Regent Concert Orchestra (BH 1922).

6. St. Agnes' Eve, Incidental Music. Nos. 1 and 2 only.
   Regent Concert Orchestra (BH 1909).

7. Minnehaha Suite, op. 82, no. 2. The Pursuit and the
   Homecoming, arranged and orchestrated by P. Fletcher. Regent Concert Orchestra (BH 1916).

8. Onaway! Awake, Beloved. Tenor solo, Webster Booth
   (G-C3407). Also, J. McHugh (CDX 1512). Also, T.
   Davies (GD 1142). Also, F. Titterton (DK 543).

9. Petite Suite de Concert, op. 77. Royal Marines Or-
   chestra, cond. Dunn (C-DX1041/2). Also, Queen's
   Hall Light Orchestra, cond. Torch (CDB 2479/80).
   Also, London Symphony Orchestra, cond. Sargent
   (G-C2372/3) Vic. 11283/4. Also, Bournemouth Mu-
   nicipal Orchestra, cond. Godfrey (C-DX651/2).

10. Suite from the Incidental Music to Othello, op. 79.
    New Symphony, cond. Sargent (GB 4273/4).

11. Sonata in D Minor, op. 28 for violin and piano (pre-
    1936 recording). A. Catterall and W. Murdoch (CL
    1396/7).

12. The Songs of Hiawatha, op. 30: Hiawatha's Wedding Feast (pre-1936). Royal Choral Society with the Albert Hall Orchestra, cond. Sargent, with tenor Walter Glynne. (G-C1931/4).

13. Three Dream Dances, op. 74, no. 2. London Palladium Orchestra, cond. Greenwood (GB 8876/7 and Vic. 27230/1).

14. Three Fours Valse Suite, op. 71. No. 1 in A-flat major and no. 6 in C Minor. Arranged for orchestra. Palm Concert Orchestra, cond. Sandler (C-D82212).

15. Viking Song, arr. Fletcher for men's chorus (TTBB) (pre-1936 recording). Associated Glee Clubs (ZON G 076).

SONGS

1. Big Lady Moon (pre-1936 recording). V. Oppenshaw, alto (GB 688).

2. Eléanore, op. 37, no. 6. Henry Wendon, tenor, and Gerald Moore, pianist (C-DB2083). Also H. Wendon, tenor, H. Greenslade, piano (GB 9451). Also R. Henderson (DF 1699). Also T. Davies (GD 1273).

3. Life and Death. Webster Booth, tenor and Hubert Greenslade, piano (G-B9451).

4. Sons of the Sea (pre-1936 recording). P. Dawson (GC 2728).

5. This Is the Island of Gardens (pre-1936 recording). A. Richless (GB 8285).

6. Thou Art Risen, My Beloved. T. Layton, tenor, accompanied by himself (CFB 3031).

7. Thou Has Bewitched Me, Beloved (pre-1936 recording). A. Richless (GB 8285).

8. Unmindful of the Roses, op. 57, no. 5 (pre-1936 recording). Webster Booth, tenor, and Hubert Greenslade, piano. (G-B9451). Also, A. Richless (GB 572).

RECORDINGS THAT ARE ON TAPE AT THE INSTITUTE OF
RECORDED SOUND, LONDON

1. Famous British Tenors, EMI Record (HOM 1228 or IE
   053. 00886m). Band 7: "Elĕanore," op. 27, no. 7.
   Henry Wendon, tenor, Gerald Moore, piano. Re-
   corded June, 1942 [Wendon (1900-1964) was leading
   tenor at Sadler's Wells in the 1930's.] Band 8:
   "Onaway! Awake, Beloved." Recorded July, 1926.
   Tudor Davies, with orchestra accompaniment.
   [Davies (1892-1958) was a leading tenor with the Old
   Vic, Sadler's, and Carl Rosa Opera Companies.]

2. British Concert Pops, George Weldon conducting the
   Philharmonia and Pro Arte Orchestra. The disc in-
   cludes the Petite Suite de Concert (EMI SXLP 30123)
   (IE 047- 04296).

3. "Sweet Evenings Come and Go."   Sung by Walter Hyde
   (1875-1951).   (Rubini GV 5.)

4. John McCormack, Songs by Bax, Brahms, Elgar, Rach-
   maninoff, Schubert, Vaughan Williams, Wolf, Coleridge-Taylor. "She Rested by the Broken Brook,"
   with Edwin Schneider, piano. Recorded July 23,
   1935 (EMI HOM 1176).

5. Alma Gluck sings Dawn by Taylor. (Rococo 5291.)

SUGGESTED LISTS OF RECORD SPECIALISTS IN ENGLAND

James H. Crawley
246 Church Street
Edmonton, London N99HQ

EMI Records
Hays, Middlesex

The Gramophone
177-179 Kenton Road
Harrow, Middlesex HA30HA

The Gramophone Exchange,
 Ltd.
80-82 Wardour Street
London WIV 4BD

The Old Record
12 May Road
Twickenham

Appendix E

BIBLIOGRAPHY

Aldrich, Richard. Concert Life in New York, 1902-1923.
New York: G. P. Putnam's Sons, 1941.

Antcliffe, Herbert. "Some Notes on Coleridge-Taylor."
Musical Quarterly (New York), vol. 8, no. 2, (April
1922).

Aronowsky, S. Performing Times of Orchestral Works.
London: Ernest Benn, 1959.

Blom, Eric, ed. Grove's Dictionary of Music and Musicians. New York: St. Martin's Press, 1973.

British Broadcasting Corporation. BBC Chamber Music
Catalogue. London: BBC Music Library, 1967.

_____. BBC Choral and Opera Catalogue. London: BBC
Music Library, 1967.

_____. BBC Piano Catalogue. London: BBC Music Li-
brary, 1967.

Clough, Francis F., and Cumming, G. J. World's Encyclopedia of Recorded Sound. London: Sidgwick and
Jackson, 1952.

Coleridge-Taylor, Avril. "My Father and His Music."
Fanfare (Birmingham, Eng.), 1948.

_____. "Samuel Coleridge-Taylor." Music and Musi-
cians (London), August, 1975.

Coleridge-Taylor, Jessie Fleetwood. A Memory Sketch of

215

Personal Reminiscences of My Husband, Genius and Musician. London: privately published, 1943.

DuBois, W. E. B. The Soul of Black People. Chicago: A. C. McClurg and Co., 1903.

Dunbar, Paul Laurence. The Complete Poems. New York: Dodd, Mead and Co., 1965.

_____. Lyrics of Love and Laughter. New York: Dodd, Mead and Co., 1903.

_____. Lyrics of Lowly Life. New York: Dodd, Mead and Co., 1896.

Foster, Miles Burkitt. The History of the Philharmonic Society of London, 1813-1912. London: John Lane, 1912.

Gramophone Shop Encyclopedia of Recorded Music. New York: Crown Pub., 1948.

Hartnell, Phyllis, ed. The Oxford Companion to the Theatre. London: Oxford University Press, 1967.

Johns, Altona Trent. "Teaching Coleridge-Taylor's 'They Will Not Lend Me a Child'." Staff Notes (Midland Park, N.J.), vol. 15, no. 1 (Spring 1976).

Longfellow, Henry Wadsworth. The Song of Hiawatha. The Frederic Remington Illustrated Edition. New York: Bounty Books [rept. of 1890 ed.].

Lovell, John, Jr. Black Song. New York: Macmillan, 1972.

Nardone, Thomas R.; Nye, James H.; and Resnick. Choral Music in Print: Vol. I, Sacred Choral Music. Philadelphia: Musicdata, Inc., 1974.

_____; _____; and _____. Choral Music in Print: Vol. II, Secular Choral Music. Philadelphia: Musicdata, Inc., 1974.

Sayers, W. C. Berwick. Samuel Coleridge-Taylor, Musician: His Life and Letters. London: Cassell, 1915.

Southern, Eileen. The Music of Black Americans. New York: W. W. Norton & Co., 1971.

_____. Readings in Black American Music. New York: W. W. Norton & Co., 1971.

Tortolano, William. "Samuel Coleridge-Taylor." Music / The AGO and RCCO Magazine, August 1975.

Williams, C. Lee, and Chance, H. Goodwin. Annals of the Three Choirs of Gloucester, Hereford and Worcester: Continuation of Progress from 1895-1922. Gloucester, Eng.: Chance and Bland, Ltd., n.d.

Young, Percy. "Samuel Coleridge-Taylor, 1875-1912." Musical Times (London), August 1975.

INDEX